# AUTO ACCIDENT PERSONAL INJURY INSURANCE CLAIM

## (How To Evaluate and Settle Your Loss)

By

Dan Baldyga

ISBN: 1-5882-0574-6  (e-book)
ISBN: 1-5882-0328-X  (Paperback)

Library of Congress Control  Number: 2001126216

This book is printed on acid free paper.


Printed in the United States of America
Bloomington, IN

1stBooks – rev. 11/25/02

**To Diane, my amazing wife of over 40 years - - the creator of our spectacular family - - Sharon, Mark, Lisa and Scott. Diane, you are the love of my life, my reality check and my best critic.**

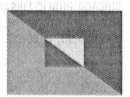

# ACKNOWLEDGMENTS

For some time now, I've been determined to help every person I can who, after being involved in a motor vehicle accident, is struggling with the problem of how to position themselves so nobody would take advantage of them. I believe this book, my Formula and the program I've detailed on the following pages have accomplished that.

There's no way I could have put this project together alone. When one attempts to develop a game plan such as this there are always so many people to thank who helped make it become a reality.

I shall always remain deeply indebted to my beautiful and talented daughter Sharon A. Macmillan MD, my crackerjack of an editor Toni Brandmill and so many other gifted individuals including that master of the creative process Shel Horowitz, in addition to Dan Scontras, Cathy Miller and Anna Kleeberg.

I would also like to thank a legion of informative and enlightened voices from the past including Ed Dolan, Norm Tower and Johnny Brogan plus a number of wise, professional and highly competent adjusters and attorneys.

And last, but certainly not least, I wish to acknowledge my son Mark for his sweat and toil on this project. I shall always be thankful for his outstanding assistance, incredible input and professional wisdom!

So, to all those super and generous people mentioned above, please accept my most profound and heartfelt "thank you." There's no way I could have done put this together without you.

# Contents

# Appendixes

The following pages will provide the reader with the know-how needed to determine the value of a personal injury claim *plus* the expertise to bring it to a successful conclusion. It is not a legal text, nor should it be considered one.

## AN INITIAL WORD ABOUT THE USE OF THIS BOOK

Many people involved in a motor vehicle accident think only of contacting their own insurance company to make a claim for repair of their property damage. They do not automatically think about filing a claim for personal injury including "pain and suffering" against the insurance of the person who hit them. This is especially true since the advent of so-called "no fault" insurance. While it is true that in "no-fault" States the PIP (Personal Injury Protection) coverage may set forth certain conditions or limits to personal injury claims, there are circumstances under which you may claim damages for personal injury even in these states. These are explained in further detail in Chapter Eleven of this book.

## 1. HANDLING AND EVALUATING YOUR CLAIM

Can you handle and evaluate your insurance claim if you have no legal background? Of course you can! The facts are that 48% of all auto accidents are rear-enders, and 99% of rear-enders are the fault of the driver who struck you. Considering that mathematical certainty, then adding to it the data which proves that in the vast majority of motor vehicle accidents it's obvious who is responsible for the carnage, it becomes clear that a knowledge of the law isn't necessary for you to satisfactorily resolve your loss.

This book will guide you through the insurance claim wilderness. It's loaded with invaluable insights. Not only will it reveal the inside secrets of claim negotiating but it will also show you how to settle your case for top dollar.

## 2. WHAT YOUR COMPENSATORY DAMAGES ARE WORTH

Your "Compensatory Damages" are what is defined by law as your "pain and suffering." Compensatory Damages will be referred to as "pain and suffering" throughout the book.

Statistics reveal that in the year 2001 there were 12 million motor vehicle accidents in The United States involving 21 million vehicles. (This amounts to approximately one crash per second). These 12 million accidents produced well over 6 million injuries. Each year these figures increase.

The inside information in this book will position you to correctly evaluate your personal injury insurance claim. It is geared to help those millions of people who have a case of clear liability. Knowing how to guide an accident claim to a victorious payoff is not an exclusive ability, possessed by a select few. Don't be seduced into thinking you can't do it yourself. That simply isn't true! This book will show you how.

The mystery of how to place a value on your "pain and suffering" has been solved with the introduction of **BASE: The Baldyga Auto Accident Settlement Evaluation Formula.** This formula, developed over many years of settling auto insurance claims on behalf of the insurance companies, is now made available to the average consumer who needs it more than my former erstwhile employers. If you document your losses, and know how to present them, then choosing which of the 4 values that **BASE** provides for you, either The PREMIUM Value (high value), The MEAN Value (high-medium value), The CORE Value (mid-value), or The LOW Value (low value), is not difficult to decide. **BASE** is a simple, easy to learn, yet revolutionary 21st Century evaluation tool.

Once you understand and implement **BASE** it will be clear to the adjuster assigned to your case that you have a solid handle on the value of your claim and (unlike most claimants) you know exactly what you're doing. When this reality has been established, your claim will take on a new complexion. Contrary to what you might think, this will provide the adjuster with a sense of relief. Why? Because he will know that the amount of money the two of you will ultimately settle for will not have been arrived at by subterfuge, concealment, undue aggressiveness, or other such unpalatable tactics, but rather by means of intelligent negotiations. That's a breath of fresh air blowing through the typical insurance adjusters work life and will help you to settle your claim for the absolute highest amount.

## 3. THE UNINFORMED CLAIMANT

The uninformed claimant has a vague understanding of his rights and obligations. He has little or no concept of the ultimate value of his possible recovery. Because of this he's less able to make appropriate demands. As the claims negotiation process moves towards a close his settlement demands are very often *too low* or *too high*. He's ignorant of the accepted principles that justify his demands. When he attempts to negotiate with these handicaps he runs a strong chance of being victimized.

## 4. THE INSURANCE COMPANY'S POINT OF VIEW

In a case where their insured is clearly responsible for an accident, settling the claim, rather than refusing to pay it, is advantageous to the insurance company. It's cheaper for them to pay than to prolong the fight because it's an indisputable fact that the longer an adjuster works on a claim the more money his company ends up spending. And, statistics reflect, if the claim goes to court, their costs will skyrocket.

Once an insurance company knows it's likely they'll have to pay your claim, somewhere  down the line (because you understand how much it's worth and will not choose to disappear empty-handed), it makes financial sense for them to pay you sooner, rather than later. This is especially true when the fault for the accident is obviously that of their insured.

Settling an injury claim with an insurance company is quite simple. You don't need to comprehend technical language or complex legalisms. Your right to be adequately compensated depends on nothing more than common sense. In a case where you're not at fault the issue simply comes down to "how much" you're going to be paid.

The amount of compensation you should receive isn't found in a crystal ball. Rather, a number of simple factors - type of accident, injuries, medical costs, lost wages - go into determining how much a claim is worth. The amount an insurance company is willing to pay actually falls into a fairly narrow spectrum. You'll know what that range is because **The Baldyga Auto Accident Settlement Evaluation Formula (BASE)** will tell you. When the insurance adjuster realizes that you understand the claims process and also understand that you know how much your "pain and suffering" is worth (thanks to **BASE**), he'll want to settle your claim and move on as soon as possible.

---

## SUMMING UP

To read this book is to become informed on bodily injury insurance claim settlement facts and details. You'll discover how to implement **BASE** so you can determine the value of the "pain and suffering" you endured because of your injury; you'll know what to ask for and how to negotiate it; and you'll supply the adjuster with all the documentation and proof needed to establish your claim. You'll learn how to do this on the following pages.

If you proceed as instructed you will not be taken advantage of, and I believe you will walk away from the negotiation table with a smile on your face.

13

# DISCLAIMER

The Publisher and Author have researched all information contained in this manual to ensure its accuracy. Nevertheless, details of laws, rules, or procedures change from time to time, especially with respect to adjustment and settlement of personal injury claims and damages sustained in automobile accidents. Further, details of rules of procedures often differ from one state or locality to another. This relatively short manual is intended as a general guide and is not intended to be an encyclopedia or to contain the answer to every issue on the subject.

**THE READER IS THEREFORE FOREWARNED THAT THIS MANUAL IS SOLD AND DISTRIBUTED WITH THIS DISCLAIMER:** The publisher and/or author neither make nor imply any guarantee of any type whatsoever as to the validity of any information contained herein nor in any other regard whatsoever.

The information contained herein is provided to assist the reader in determining a value for his claim. However, it is obviously not suggested that the claim amount considered after applying the material in this book is the absolute maximum amount that could possibly have been obtained in a court of law or otherwise. Neither the publisher nor author purport to render any type of professional or legal service whatsoever or to substitute for a lawyer, an accountant, financial planner, an insurance adjuster or claims consultant, or the like. Where such professional help is called for in your specific or other cases, it should be sought accordingly.

# Executive Summary

Auto Accident Personal Injury Insurance Claim

Daniel G. Baldyga

© 2002

*I urge you to read the book in its entirety. It reads easily and takes a reasonably short time to complete. If you are one of those people who wants "the bottom line" you're in luck as well. I have prepared a special **Executive Summary** that outlines the key issues of the book in just a few pages. Obviously, this is not intended to take the place of reading the entire book. However, it serves as a good introduction to the key concepts.*                                                     *Dan Baldyga*

## INTRODUCTION

Nearly 50% of motor vehicle accidents are rear-enders. These are generally accepted in the industry (and by the courts) as being the fault of the person who hit the car in front of them. In most of these cases a lawyer is not needed to settle the case. Most people do not know how many dollars their personal injury is worth nor understand the range of values it falls within. That always provides insurance adjusters with a huge advantage. This book will show you how to place a value on your "pain and suffering" and position you to negotiate a good settlement.

## CHAPTER ONE: FIRST THINGS FIRST

Chapter One explains who you should notify after the accident, and includes a list of what to do (and not do) when you contact your insurance company and when you talk to the other driver and their insurance company.

Examples include: Do not admit responsibility; do not agree to provide a written or recorded statement; remain calm and polite to all parties; do not offer any details about the accident or about your injuries; do not rush to settlement too quickly; and be sure to check the statute of limitations for your State so you know how long you will have to file a lawsuit if it eventually comes down to threatening legal action.

## CHAPTER TWO: YOU WERE THE VICTIM OF A TORT

Chapter Two explains that a tort is a civil wrong (such as when someone hits you) and that you were the victim of a tort. It covers parent and spouse obligations: parents have certain obligations for their children and spouses have certain obligations for each other. You can expect compensation for the harm done to you and your property. In addition, you should be paid for "pain and suffering" the injury caused.

## CHAPTER THREE: GATHERING ACCIDENT FACTS

Eye witnesses are invaluable. You should work hard at identifying them and this chapter gives you dozens of examples and ideas on how to do just that. Do not dismiss the value of family and/or friends as witnesses – they can be very helpful as well. Photographs are essential. They can greatly increase the value of your claim . You can sometimes obtain photos from the local newspaper and the police department. Photos worth obtaining include skid marks, crash evidence, damage to your property including your car, physical damage, and color photographs of scars and injuries (these are especially helpful at raising the value of a claim).

## CHAPTER FOUR: DAMAGES

Damages include the damage to your car – and "Special Damages". **Special Damages** are the primary focus of this chapter and they are critical to understanding the value of your claim. It is these damages – not the damage to your motor vehicle – that will get multiplied and factored into **The BASE Formula** to increase the value of your claim. Chapter Four includes a long check list for you but, in summary, there are "Medical Special Damages" such as the costs for an ambulance, medication *including over-the-counter medications*, physical therapy, creams and lotions, doctor and hospital bills, etc. and there are also "Non-Medical Special Damages" that get multiplied to add value your claim. These include things such as the value of your lost wages *(even if you have been paid by your employer!) and based on your gross wages before tax* – plus travel, household help, and child care. Also discussed are property damages including a right to claim rental car costs.

## CHAPTER FIVE: PROPERTY DAMAGE

"Actual Cash Value" is the basis of your property damage. This means that your vehicle will be valued as "depreciated" (and is probably worth less than you think). You can check out a car's value in the Kelly Blue Book available online or in print . However, "standard guides" often used by an adjuster are not absolute and if a guidebook figure seems too low, you may refuse to accept it. When submitting repair costs, a good adjuster will look for replacement of parts not damaged by the accident, replacement of parts caused by wear and tear, charges for "new" parts where used parts were installed, overcharges on parts, duplication of parts and labor, inclusion of previous damage in the new damage estimate and incorrect addition. You can settle the property damage portion of a claim separately from the personal injury portion. However, before cashing your property damage settlement check, be sure it is written as "Property Damage Only", do NOT deposit any check or sign any release that states "General release" and be sure to insist that the adjuster indicates "Property Damage Only" on the check.

## CHAPTER SIX:  YOUR BODILY INJURY

This Chapter explains in great detail, various types of injuries and their relation to your claim.  Included are discussions about strain and stress, anxiety, hard injuries, muscles, arthritis, joints, scars, and so forth.  Whiplash is discussed as well since the term is often misunderstand and associated with fraud.  However, whiplash injuries are common and painful and this chapter explains what you can do to document the symptoms properly.   Pain and Suffering is discussed in this Chapter as well.  It is noted that certain types of individuals (such as professional athletes) may be expected to have a higher "pain threshold" than other types of people.

## CHAPTER SEVEN:  INSURANCE ADJUSTERS

Most insurance adjusters are reasonably fair and are a bit distrustful partly as a result of years dealing with people who are lying or trying to take advantage of a claim.  They are overworked and are usually as eager as you to settle your case and get it off their plate.   If you have your facts in order and are firm but calm you can maximize your claim.    Never underestimate the value of the adjuster's impressions and conclusions about you.   When you are first contacted, avoid giving the impression that you are fully recovered.  Be polite but not overly friendly.   Do not agree to sign anything or to make a statement, either written or recorded, until your claim has been settled to an amount satisfactory to you.  When you meet the adjuster, bring along a friend to act as a witness and to keep the meeting professional and keep the adjuster from trying to manipulate the conversation.  You do not need to agree to be examined by their doctor unless the claim ends up in court.

## CHAPTER EIGHT:  THE BASE FORMULA

Your personal injury claim will generally be worth between two to four times the amount of your "special damages" (see Chapter Four).   The minimum claim settlement target (excluding property damage) is typically at least two times Special Damages (we call this the "Low Value").   A reasonable solid target would be either three times Special Damages (the "Core Value") or three and a half times Special Damages (the "Mean Value").   In some cases, you can shoot for four times Special Damages (the "Premium Value").

The ranges and reasons behind which value will apply to your particular case are explained in this chapter.  They include such issues as the age,  profession, driving record, and character profile of yourself and the other driver.   Also to be considered are photographs, scars, and other such matters. The chapter includes various examples of **The BASE Formula** in action.

## CHAPTER NINE: HOW TO NEGOTIATE WITH AN ADJUSTER

Determine the value and ask for double that amount. That's a good high starting point and puts the adjuster on the defensive. Do not lower your demand until the adjuster makes a counter-offer. Think of the negotiating process as similar to selling a car or any other property. You initially ask for more than you're willing to accept and the potential buyer offers less than they're willing to pay. Be patient. You do not need to settle the claim in the first meeting. Be straight and avoid verbal abuse.

## CHAPTER TEN: STALEMATE

You'll usually find an adjuster's supervisor willing to chat. One of his major responsibilities is to reduce his department's claim load. The mere mention of filing a complaint with the state department of insurance may help. If not, consider actually filing a complaint. This may cause your case to come to the attention of someone in the insurance company other than the adjuster and inspire a better offer. If you cannot resolve it there, consider small claims court. Check your state's maximum limit. This Chapter explains how to prepare for small claims court. Often the threat of a lawsuit and the start of that process is enough to bring the case to settlement.

## CHAPTER ELEVEN: NO-FAULT INSURANCE

No-Fault insurance (Personal Injury Protection or PIP) is applicable in about half of the States. However, whether or not your state has PIP included in your insurance policy, there are several circumstances under which you can still make a personal injury claim outside of the limits imposed by that system. These are explained in detail in this Chapter. In some states, there is a monetary threshold that must be met. Every state varies so it is essential to check the specific limits of your state.

## CHAPTER TWELVE: SOME VARIOUS INSIGHTS

Chapter Twelve explains various insurance coverage such as Property Damage Liability Coverage (your damage to someone else's property) , Comprehensive Coverage (flood, hail, fire, theft, vandalism), Collision Coverage (repair to your damage), Uninsured and Underinsured Motorist Coverage (pays for you and your passenger's medical expenses, pain and suffering, etc. caused by an uninsured or underinsured driver), Medical Payments Coverage (optional coverage to cover medical costs for you and your passengers). Also discussed is arbitration (an alternative dispute resolution to court) including the process of how to prepare for arbitration, arbitration procedures, fees, and the hearing itself.

18

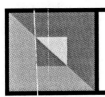

# First Things First

## 1. PROMPTLY NOTIFY

*After your accident, you should promptly notify:*

1. The Claims Departments of the drivers and owners (if the owners are different from the drivers) of all the vehicles involved in the accident. Or go directly to the drivers and/or owners themselves, especially if the insurance company(s) are unknown.

2. The insurance company of your own vehicle, whether you have Fault or No-Fault insurance coverage (CHAPTER 11) or, if you plan to make a claim under your Uninsured Motorist coverage (CHAPTER 12), your Collision Coverage or your Medical Payments Coverage.

3. The employer of the driver of any vehicle involved in the accident which might have been engaged in the business of the employer at the time of the accident.

4. Any person who may have contributed in any way to the accident, such as the property owner of an object which constituted an obstruction on the roadway, which you feel may have been either partially or totally responsible for the accident.

Notification should be in the form of a one-page letter providing only the basic facts:

The time, place, date of accident, plus the vehicles and parties involved, etc. *Your letter should refrain from any discussion of details* such as who is at fault for the accident; the injuries or physical damages you may have sustained; the claims you're going to make; and any other matters. Keep it simple, direct and to the point!

If your letter is to an individual or business, rather than to their insurance company, ask that person to refer the matter to their insurance carrier and also to promptly provide you with the name and address of that company. Your letter should be sent Certified Mail with Return Receipt Requested. It is probably unwise to correspond by e-mail, since it is difficult to know what has been received, when and by whom. Keep copies of all letters you send and receive; and make notes of all telephone conversations.

## 2. REPORTING THE ACCIDENT TO THE DEPT OF MOTOR VEHICLES

Many states have laws requiring that those involved in a motor vehicle accident causing physical injury or property damage *over a certain dollar amount* must report that accident in writing to the state's Department of Motor Vehicles. Check with your insurance agent or your local Department of Motor Vehicles to find out what the time limits are for filing this report. Sometimes you only have a few days. You should ask them whether you will need a specific form for this report.

If you must file a report and the report requests a statement about how the accident occurred, be brief. **ADMIT NO RESPONSIBILITY FOR THE ACCIDENT!**

If the form asks what your injuries are, list every one of them and not just the most serious or obvious. It is possible that an insurance company could later have access to this report. If you admitted some fault, or failed to mention an injury, you may have to explain this later on.

## 3. ACCIDENTS INVOLVING THE GOVERNMENT

Thankfully (because it's usually so complicated) it doesn't happen too often that one becomes involved with a "government" vehicle. There are *very special rules* to follow if your accident was even partially caused by a government entity like a city, county, state, federal government, or *any* public agency or division. This could include an accident with a municipal bus or a car driven by a local, state or federal employee during work hours.

Local, state and federal governments *set their own rules* regarding who can collect from them, for what and how to do it. To make a claim against a government entity you must carefully follow that state's specific rules.

There are specific time limits (usually 30 to 180 days) in which to file a claim. If you fail to do so, or don't file the required information in the proper way, you may lose your right to collect for your loss.

Because the law changes frequently, and because the process can be so complex, you should protect your interests by hiring an attorney to represent you. One who knows the "ins and outs" of how to proceed with an accident involving a government motor vehicle.

# 4. CONTACT WITH YOUR OWN INSURANCE COMPANY

Your relationship with your insurance company is established by your policy because it's a "contract" between you and your insurer. You may be obligated by the rules of the policy to provide your company with more information than you would provide to someone else's insurance company.

Some of the differences of note follow:

## 4.1. Notify Your Agent

If you give notice of the accident to your insurance agent, rather than your insurance company, it should not be more than a week before you receive a letter of confirmation. If you don't, call your insurance company directly and give them the information.

## 4.2. Right Of Subrogation

Your insurance company may send you a form entitled Right Of Subrogation. This form means if your insurance company pays you, you give them the right to recover the money, or be subrogated, from whoever else may be liable for the accident. For example, an uninsured motorist who obviously has money of his own, whom your insurance company decides to "go after" in an attempt to recover whatever they may have paid you. This right of subrogation does not affect your prerogative to collect compensation from your company, but if you file a claim under your own policy then you must agree to give subrogation to your insurer.

## 4.3. Cooperation

Most policies state that to collect on a claim under your own policy, you must cooperate with your insurance company in its investigation of the accident. If asked, you must provide the names of witnesses, the medical providers you're being treated by and a statement about how the accident happened.

# 5. CONTACT WITH THE OTHER DRIVER'S INSURANCE COMPANY

Your phone will soon be ringing. It may be an insurance adjuster, or some "inside" claims person, either of whom will be a representative of the other driver's insurance company. Here is some advice on how to handle that conversation.

## 5.1. Remain Calm And Polite

The accident you were the victim of may have upset you, but keep in mind that taking out your frustration or anger on the person calling you won't help to get properly compensated. They're only human. Nobody responds kindly to verbal abuse.

## 5.2. Provide Only Limited Personal Information

You only need to provide them with your name, address and telephone number. You can tell them what type of work you do, and where you're employed, but at this point in time you need not explain or discuss any more than that about your work or your income, etc. You're not obligated to provide any other personal information and you should keep the initial conversation brief and to the point.

## 5.3. Give No Details Of The Accident

You may be asked to dictate a statement, right then and there over the tele-phone, about how the accident happened. **Politely refuse any discussion of the facts of the accident except the most basic.** For example, tell them you would rather not discuss any facts even as basic as where and when it took place, the type of accident and the vehicles involved. Tell them you will discuss the facts further, at the appropriate time. Do not commit yourself to identifying wit-nesses you know of or offering witness statements should you have acquired some (See Chapter 3). However, if they do get into that subject matter, take a shot and ask if *they* know of any witnesses. Maybe they'll tell you!

### 5.4. Provide No Details Of Your Injuries

The person on the other end of the phone will want to know about your injuries. It is not wise to give them any detailed description. It's much too early. Be cautious. Holding your injury information "close to the vest" is the only route you should take because you may leave something out, or discover an injury later, or your injury may evolve into something much worse than you originally thought. Advise them you'll be seeking or continuing medical treatment. There's no law or rule that says you have to tell them what doctors or medical providers you're seeing, and you should not provide that yet.

### 5.5. Resist A Rush To Settlement

Claims people sometimes try to offer a settlement during the first one or two phone calls. Quick settlements like that save the insurance company work and, more importantly, gets you to settle for a much smaller figure before you've been able to determine what your "pain and suffering" is worth. This dollar amount will be determined later, when all the facts are known, by your implementation of **The BASE Formula** (Chapter 8). A "quickie" settlement will almost certainly cost you money, perhaps *a lot of money!*

### 5.6. Limit Your Conversations

Let the person you're talking to know that until you've finished gathering all the facts regarding the accident, been discharged from your doctor and are fully recovered from your injuries, you'd rather not discuss how the accident happened, the extent of your injuries or what a settlement figure should be.

In some situations it may not be practical to stop all phone conversations. For example, you may need to discuss repairs to your car. If you do speak to that person, and/or the adjuster, you should set the limits on the place and time (your home or at work - morning or evening, etc.) for contact.

It's important to remember that until you've had an opportunity to investigate, plus determine the extent and duration of your injuries and how long it will take to recover from them, you won't have any accurate information to offer.

### 5.7. Do not sign anything!

Not only should you not sign any documents whatsoever, but before you provide *anybody* with information about your accident there are a number of fundamentals you should review so you're confident all the essentials are covered. (Basic checklists of those benchmarks can be found in both APPENDIX A: Initial Personal Checklist Regarding Your Accident and APPENDIX D: After Impact Checklist).

## STATUTE OF LIMITATIONS

You only have a certain amount of time in which to collect for your loss. The law of the state where the accident occurred is the one that controls the statute, *regardless of the state in which you live.* Watch the time! It will begin to run on the date of the accident. Especially if you are getting close to one year from the date of your accident, you *must* double check the Statute of Limitations *in the state where your accident took place,* to determine its latest version. See APPENDIX B Statute of Limitations but double-check— because laws change!

| You Were The Victim Of A Tort | Auto Accident Personal Injury Insurance Claim |
|---|---|
| | **CHAPTER 2** |
| | © 2002 Daniel G. Baldyga |

## I. WHAT IS A TORT?

A tort is a misdeed! It's a wrongful act for which relief may be obtained in the form of money. The subject of torts is the understanding of the rights of the individual and the relief available to them should these rights be violated. A tort has been defined as a civil wrong. For the purposes of this book, a tort should be thought of as a claim for property damage or bodily injury arising out of, or sustained as a result of, an accident stemming from the negligence of another.

For example, the witness to your accident said, "That guy was at a dead stop. The other driver came along at a high rate of speed and hit him a tremendous whack in the rear end. I saw the guy's head snap forward and backward like a whipsaw. He smashed his face on the steering wheel, broke his nose. Blood all over the place. Man, what a mess!" *That* is the grounds for a solid tort!

Generally speaking every person who violates the personal or property rights of another is financially responsible for the damages caused by his or her act. To collect for this civil wrong there *must* be damages and/or injury; without these, there can be no recovery of money. Whenever you or your property has been wrongfully harmed or injured, by someone else's actions, you're said to have suffered a *tort*. The wrongdoer is usually identified as the *tort-feasor*.

Based on the doctrine of tort, it's held that under any given circumstance, each and every individual owes the other a legal duty, which exists by virtue of society's expectations regarding interpersonal conduct, rather than by contract or other private relationship. When someone commits a breach of this duty - that is, they fail to observe or respect another's entitlement to this duty - then that person has committed a civil tort against the wronged party.

## 2. WHO IS RESPONSIBLE?

Under normal circumstances the person who commits a tort is legally responsible for all damages which flow directly, or indirectly, from his tortuous act - provided such damage is the "proximate" cause, or can be attributed to the act. In most states infants cannot bring an action in their own name. In the event of a pending full-blown court action an infant must bring the action through his "next friend" who is generally his father or mother.

25                                                    © 1999-2003 Daniel G. Baldyga

## 3. MINORS AND PARENTS AND FAMILY

The parents of an injured minor may have the obligation to provide necessary medical treatment and will, therefore, have a claim for that expense. They are also entitled to the services of the minor children and, in some very rare instances, may have a claim for the value of services lost.

The husband has an obligation to provide necessary medical treatment for an injured wife and has a claim for that expense. In some states he is also entitled to consortium, which is defined as "...the sex, service and society of his wife." As chauvinistic as it may sound, the husband may have a claim for any interference with this right. In some states a wife may also have a claim for the loss of consortium of her husband.

Proof of the above may raise the value of your claim and may raise the value of your claim "up a level" when using **The BASE Formula**. Remember, there are four levels provided for in **The BASE Formula**. These are the Low Value, Core Value, Mean Value and Premium Value (See Chapter Eight). Furthermore, even if it did not by itself warrant moving from one level to the next, it would certainly go a long way in justifying the "Value" you've decided to aim for. See Chapter Eight for more on "Values" and **The BASE Formula**.

## 4. WHAT FINANCIAL REWARDS CAN YOU EXPECT?

Automobile accident awards, in the form of money, are your compensation for the harm done to you and your property. FOR EXAMPLE: You were injured in an automobile accident due to the negligent operation of a motor vehicle by another. You're entitled to recover your lost wages, medical bills, property damage and all other out-of-pocket expenses. *In addition,* the law states you should recover compensatory damages - for the "pain and suffering" your injury caused you.

## 5. BASIC RULES OF LIABILITY

The rules of liability are not complicated. They require nothing more than common sense. Liability revolves around the simple fact that most accidents happen because someone was careless - or negligent.

This book has nothing to do with establishing liability. We accept as a given that a person who hit you from behind is responsible for the accident. This book is about the evaluation of a personal injury, and how to execute **The BASE Formula**. **BASE** will reveal how much money the "pain and suffering" you've endured is worth.

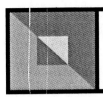

| Gathering Accident Facts | Auto Accident Personal Injury Insurance Claim |
| --- | --- |
| | **CHAPTER 3** |
| | © 2002 Daniel G. Baldyga |

This book is about you, the faultless individual. Blameless because the person who struck you is 100% responsible for the damage they have caused you. When the liability for a motor vehicle accident is clear it's not necessary to do all that is suggested in this fairly long chapter. However, like good old fashioned chicken soup, it can't hurt! Besides, what you may discover can and often *will* raise the value of your claim.

## 1. THE EYE WITNESS

Not only can a witness substantiate who was at fault in a motor vehicle accident but in many instances a witness can and does add double-barreled value to your personal injury claim. The adjuster knows that a strong statement by a witness (especially one which will cause a jury to cringe when they hear, in specific detail, about the tremendous shock your body was subjected to) could greatly increase the amount of money that jury agrees to pay for your "pain and suffering."

As far back as 1968, in my book *How To Settle Your Own Insurance Claim*, I stated, *"An eye witness can make or break your case. If you have been able to keep your wits about you the first thing you should do, immediately after the accident has occurred, is to find somebody who saw it. If you do spot someone, don't be bashful. Go right over to him or her and ask if they saw the accident. If they did, jot down their name, address and telephone number. If they drive away before you can zero in on them, make note of the license plate number on their vehicle so later on you can try to find them through the department of motor vehicle office."* What I wrote over 30 years ago remains true today. Very little has changed over the past *sixty* years!

### 1.1. Utilizing The Witness

The "witness person" could be somebody who was walking or standing nearby, a passenger in your own or other vehicles, or drivers of motor vehicles not directly involved in the accident.

#### 1.1.1. Time Is Of The Essence
If there is one it's important you get to that person as soon as possible. By moving quickly you stand the best chance of getting them committed to your account of the events and/or to come down on your side of the case. Time is of the essence. If witnesses aren't contacted, and their information confirmed right after the accident, what they have to say can be lost forever. Memories fade and recollections become fuzzy. Also, if you wait too long, you may discover a witness has moved out of the area.

© 1999-2003 Daniel G. Baldyga

1.1.2. <u>Contact With The Witness</u>

Contact each witness (identified from the list of persons you compiled at the accident scene - or perhaps found in the police report) and talk to them about what they saw or know, concerning the accident. The ideal procedure is to get them to write out, in detail, what they observed, in their own words. If they're not willing to do this, then write a statement yourself, of what each witness tells you, then ask them to sign and date it. Try to capture their recollections, impressions and observations of what happened. If the statement is more than one page, have them initial and date the bottom of each page, then sign it in full at the end. Make a copy and send it to them. Do this so they'll know exactly what they told you if, at a later date, it becomes important for them to remember.

## 1.2. Dealing With A Stranger-Witness

People who you don't know can be helpful to your claim. They may have observed the accident and/or reveal something useful you hadn't considered. If you find a witness keep in mind the following:

1. Write down their names, their mail and e-mail address and, if possible, both their home and work phone numbers.

2. Chat with them about what they saw. Ask them exactly where they were when they observed what happened.

3. If a witness seems to cooperate, ask if it would be alright if you had somebody type up what they're telling you - then go over it with them for accuracy. If they agree, jot down what they say. Later, bring them that statement typed, and politely ask them to review and sign it.

4. If they are uncomfortable to "get involved" jot down their comments and ask them to read what they told you to make sure it's accurate. Be sure you have their correct address or telephone number so you can later prove what you have is from a living, breathing person.

## 1.3. Witnesses You Know Personally

If a friend, relative or acquaintance witnessed your accident, your job is essentially the same as with the stranger. Be sure to review the facts with them while their memory is fresh. Make notes of what they tell you. Then, as soon as possible, provide them with a typed statement and have them sign it. Personal friends, or relatives, as a witness, can be crucial. Don't ever let anybody tell you because your witness is a personal friend it will diminish the value of their observations. Not true! There are hundreds of thousands of well settled motor vehicle accident claims on record that prove this to be false. Their value as a witness can be monumental.

### 1.4. Should The Witness Also Talk To The Adjuster?

The decision whether to talk to the adjuster should be left up to each witness. In this way, they can remain independent and therefore believable.

### 1.5. The Missing Witness

You may be unable to directly contact or locate the whereabouts of a witness whose name, home address or phone number you've obtained. The witness may have moved. Here are two suggestions on how to find a witness:

1.  Send a Certified or Registered letter to the witness, addressed to his or her last known address, with the Return Receipt Requested and the Addressee Only boxes checked off. If you then receive back from the post office the Return Receipt, signed by the witness, or executed by the post office, you should find entered thereon, the current address of the witness.

2.  If you have their full name and address, and you're comfortable surfing the Internet, there are a multitude of methods to locate them. Should you not be wise to the ways of cyber-space find somebody who is to help you. To familiarize yourself with one of the many procedures one can implement to find a witness see APPENDIX C: Locating A Missing Witness.

---

## IN SUMMARY REGARDING WITNESSES

I spent more than half my life investigating motor vehicle accidents - first as a private investigator working my way through college while representing several insurance companies, handling their motor vehicle accidents, later as a Special Investigator in the United States Navy covering incredibly serious accidents throughout the Mid-West, and then over thirty years as a claims adjuster, supervisor and manager. I know from personal experience that a witness to a motor vehicle accident can be invaluable in helping to make a case.

Witnesses can describe things in an accident that confirm what you believe happened, thus backing up your story. Or they may provide you with information of which you weren't even vaguely aware. For example, a witness may have overheard a verbal remark, from the driver who hit you, admitting their fault.

## 2. PHOTOGRAPHS

In the world of insurance claims, photographs of the accident scene, the property damage to the vehicle, injuries, or other related matters, are viewed as the finest evidence and very often the most substantial proof that you, the claimant, could possibly have. They can prove your innocence *and also* increase the value of your claim.

---

A camera is one of the best tools to assist you in obtaining a fair settlement of your accident claim for the following reasons:

1. Photos preserve scenes, evidence and personal injuries that are guaranteed to change over time.

2. Photos usually capture facts much better than you could ever describe them.

3. Photos often reveal details you would have not noticed with the naked eye.

4. Photos are *dramatic!* They highlight whatever they're focused on, without the distractions of surrounding sounds and sights.

5. Photos cannot be contradicted. It's impossible to deny what is documented by a photograph.

6. Photos help you to focus on the important points you wish to make. Remember it's *you* who selects which photos to show the adjuster.

7. Photos will impress the adjuster. They will demonstrate to him that you're an organized and highly competent individual, one who knows what he's doing and will not be conned.

---

### 2.1. Why Take Photographs?

Photos of your motor vehicle will help you to establish and justify:

1. How hard you were hit and the mighty impact your motor vehicle, *and your body,* sustained.

2. The amount of your medical bills, the length of your partial and/ or total disability and the period of time you were unable to work. (These critical factors are discussed in CHAPTER 6: YOUR BODILY INJURY).

## 2.2. How To Take Photos

When you photograph the scene of the accident do so at approximately the same time of day and the same day of the week as your accident occurred (unless, of course, it was past sunset). Do this so you can capture the same density and flow of traffic that normally takes place at that specific interval.

On almost every type of photo attempt you should snap at least three:

1. A general view of the subject. About 20 to 40 feet away.

2. A medium-distance view. About 10 to 15 feet away.

3. A close-up view. About 3 to 6 feet away.

These photographs should have a common point of orientation. An example of this would be a photograph of a skid mark on a paved, concrete street.

Show the skid mark in relation to some prominent and permanent landmark. A landmark can be a street sign, a building, a fire hydrant, etc. Once you've accomplished this, snap other photographs of a closer view of that skid mark, identifying it in detail. At the same moment try to include that readily identifiable object. Before snapping your photographs, consider how many photos will be required and the best angle to use. Do this to obtain maximum results.

## 2.3. How Many And What Kind Of Photographs

Usually two sets of photographs are sufficient - one for you and one to present to the adjuster. (Always retain the negatives, should you need copies later on). Don't negate the clout that will be registered on the face of the adjuster when they're presented with 8X10 colored, glossy photographs of your facial cuts, or body abrasions, or the black and blue bruise marks on your chest, etc. They'll take one look at that and *blanch*!

## 2.4. Color Photographs Of An Injury

I cannot emphasize enough the incredible value that color photographs add to a personal injury claim. Color photos, taken up close, and from different angles, are dynamite additions to your claim. They can be very dramatic and add substantially to your settlement figure. They can also justify your moving *up*, from one of the "Values" **BASE** has provided you, to another. It's almost certain that colored photographs of an injury will raise a "Value" to the next level.

## 2.5. Photographs Of Vehicles

As soon as possible, snap six to eight photos of the damage to your own motor vehicle from various angles. You should try to capture on film the condition of the other vehicle(s) as well. Possessing this particular type of evidence, in a case of clear liability, can become extremely helpful later on, when you've finally reached the point where you're deciding which of the 4 settlement "Values" you're going to aim for.

When you can manage it, try to locate the vehicle that hit you so you can snap some photos. It may have been towed to a garage in which case you might have noticed the name on the tow truck at the scene. (More often than not all the vehicles involved are towed to the same location). Also, police reports often indicate where damaged autos were taken.

## 2.6. Photographs of Skid Marks

Skid marks can be invaluable evidence since they can often indicate the speed of the vehicle at the time of the impact and therefore very useful in determining fault. Photographs can be crucial evidence in a personal injury claim, because they establish the tremendous beating your body was subjected to.

## 2.7. Newspaper Accounts

Check to see if there were newspaper accounts of the accident. If so, clip them out and save them. Also check the local newspapers as they may have written a synopsis of the weather for the day of your accident. Clip that out also. If it was a particularly bad day there may have been a headline. Save that too. Make a notation on all clippings, including the name of the newspaper, the page it appeared on and the date it was published. Place them in your file. This simple task, which takes only a moment and doesn't cost any more than the price of a newspaper, can often help when it comes time for you to determine which "Value" you're going to aim for.

I have personally observed that this sort of material proved to be an important part of the claimant's records. In an accident that took place on a dirt road, in the middle of nowhere, many miles from civilization, an insured once told me, the weather was "clear and dry" when it was actually raining cats and dogs and the visibility was almost zero. The police never came to the scene so no report was made. When I sat down with the claimant, to discuss his loss, the newspaper clipping he presented to me as proof of the weather on the day of the accident blew my insured's tall tale right out of the saddle!

After you've obtained a copy of the police report, check to find the name of the investigating officer. This is usually written on the bottom of the report. Telephone him and ask if he knows of a professional photographer who may have been at the scene. If the officer does remember give that photographer a call and ask if he has any prints for sale. Don't worry about bothering him; he'll be delighted to sell them.

Needless to say, if a photograph appeared in one of the newspapers, then it's a simple task to drive on down to the newspaper office and order an 8X10 glossy. If they have one or more photos on file they'll usually be only too happy to sell what they have. You can purchase them all or select a few.

## A WORD OF CAUTION

You or the individual engaged in the task of snapping photographs should be careful to ensure that you're not undertaking the task with a hasty or careless attitude - one that leaves it to the camera to do the thinking . Cameras don't have that capacity. If the photos are to produce the maximum results one ought to thoughtfully determine how many photos will be required and from which angles.

### IN SUMMARY REGARDING PHOTOGRAPHS

Photographs are one of the most important (in many cases *the most important*) accident facts you'll gather up to sweeten your claim and make it a success. Another advantage achieved in securing photographs is that the adjuster you'll be negotiating with will begin to comprehend he's dealing with an organized and resourceful person. He'll come to realize that you're *sharp* and you're not going to quietly disappear from the scene until you've been paid a fair and reasonable amount of money to settle your claim.

## 3. DEVELOPING A DIAGRAM OF THE ACCIDENT SCENE

The police often create a diagram as part of the Police Report — but because the officers are so busy at the scene many of these reports rarely go into much detail. A diagram depicting the accident scene and location of the street and/or intersection, etc. where the accident occurred, can be very useful. Create your own. Some major points to consider:

1.    Make a note of all compass points.

2.    Fully sketch in the locations of any and all traffic control signs.

3.    Provide as complete a description of the surrounding area as possible.

4.    Detail weather and visibility conditions at the time of the accident.

5.    Draw the measurements and locations of all pertinent objects as best you can determine them - plus the positions and lengths of all skid marks.

6.    Be sure to mark the location where the impact took place.

## 4. PHYSICAL FACTS - WHAT SPECIFICALLY TO LOOK FOR

There are many physical facts to consider, some of which have the potential to be of major significance. (See APPENDIX D: After Impact Checklist).

## 5. RETURNING TO THE SCENE

Whether the accident occurred in the area where you reside or far from home, you should return to the scene as soon as possible and attempt to locate evidence and also to photograph any conditions which may have contributed, or perhaps *caused*, the accident. You may be surprised to discover something you weren't aware of when the accident occurred, but suddenly helps to explain why it happened. For example, a traffic light that wasn't working.

## 6. THE POLICE REPORT - IF THERE IS ONE

Always call the police to the scene, *especially* if you or anybody else in your motor vehicle has been injured. It's to your advantage to do so, as the police report will be executed with that specific information in it. If you were injured, don't hold back! Complain like fury to the police of the pain you're experiencing. There is a good chance your complaint may be included as an observation in the police report; this will help you later.

In most states police are required, by law, to be promptly notified whenever an accident occurs, especially when there's an injury, or the damages to one of the vehicles is in excess of some fixed amount, for example, $250.

Whether the police are called to the accident scene or merely come upon it on their own, by law they must file a formal report. The city or county police will usually have the jurisdiction in the given area of the accident's occurrence unless the accident takes place on a state highway.

Customarily, the report will identify the names and addresses of the parties and witnesses, the names of both insurance companies, the weather and road conditions at the time of the accident and sometimes a rough diagram of the scene of the accident and other pertinent details. They rarely include their personal assessment of what caused the accident and who was at fault.

Usually, about a week after the police have executed their report, it will be available to the public. You have the right to secure a copy after paying a nominal charge.

## 7. THE UNCOMMITED POLICE REPORT

Many police reports state very little. The adjuster assigned to your case might argue "nothing in the report confirms your description of how the accident happened." In response to this you should point out to him that there's nothing in the report that contradicts your version of what happened, either. Remind him that the police officer(s) didn't witness the accident. The police officer arrived at the scene *after* the event had taken place.

Be sure to let the adjuster know, should your claim eventually end up in court, that you're aware the Police Report is of questionable value. In his heart, the adjuster will know this to be true and he'll get back to the business of bargaining.

## 8. CRASH EVIDENCE

Look for fine debris. Near the point of impact will be piles of tiny particles, such as little bits of glass, because they usually don't travel very far after being created.

Ugly holes on the highway, identified as "chop marks," can determine the point of impact. A chop mark, which is usually a gouge 1/2 to 4 inches into the road, is created by the under portion of a motor vehicle, having been forced down against the surface by the incredible pressure of one vehicle colliding with another. It's wise to make note of their location on your diagram and also to snap some photographs of them.

35

## 9. PLACE YOURSELF IN THE OTHER DRIVER'S POSITION

Get into an automobile and return to the scene. Direct your vehicle along the same path as that used by the operator of the motor vehicle that hit you. Among many other possibilities, you can usually determine the visibility they had. You may be pleasantly surprised to discover that a stop sign is obscured by shrubbery, etc. If you find something you think is extraordinary, be sure to snap many photographs of it.

## 10. SCHOOL RECORDS

When an individual works for a living then it's easier to determine (a) Lost Wages, (b) Potential lost earnings and/or (c) Lost earning capacity (See CHAPTER 4: DAMAGES). Determining lost earnings is harder if the injured person is a student.

## 11. CHECK THE RECORDS OF A CHILD OR ADULT IN SCHOOL

The school records of the claimant, when the person injured is a child or an adult in school, can be important when one attempts to judge one of **The BASE Formula's** 4 "Values." If the child's or student's symptoms are legitimate, the person reporting that to you should have no objection providing you with a short statement. A written document, containing such information, can go a long way toward justifying the "Value" you've selected, to compensate for that child or adult's, "pain and suffering."

The following checklist is a suggested guideline to follow when attempting to gather information on a student:

1. Obtain a copy of their attendance record at school, both before and after the accident. This can be a basis of comparison when negotiating with the adjuster regarding the "Value" you've decided to aim for.

2. Determine the actual time lost from school as a result of the accident.

3. Copies of their grades both before and after the accident. Physical, dental or psychological exam records the school may have on file.

4. Attitude, intelligence and/or psychological examinations and tests which may have been made prior to the accident.

5. The student's curriculum both before and after the accident.

6. Complaints the student may have verbalized to teachers, counselors, athletic directors or the principal.

7. The amount of, and type of, athletic or other extra curricular activities they may have engaged in, both before and after the accident.

36

When it comes to school records how does one determine the value of such information? That's a multi-thousand dollar question and a difficult one to answer. It's something you and the adjuster must hammer out - keeping in mind such records absolutely document a loss and, if presented to a jury, would definitely add more dollars to the bottom line. If you can prove them, that's an excellent reason to raise one of the 4 "Values" **BASE** has provided for you *up* a notch.

---

## IN SUMMARY REGARDING ACCIDENT FACTS

**BASE** is a Formula for providing the usual, normal, routine motor vehicle, bodily injury insurance claim with 4 distinct "Values" at which one can legitimately settle. But there are a multitude of circumstances where you're justified to aim for an even *higher* value. For example:

1.   The driver that smashed into you being cited for running a Stop Sign, or some other motor vehicle violation.

2.   The other driver arrested for driving under the influence of alcohol or drugs.

3.   Your age being *very young* or *very old.*

4.   Colored photographs of you showing a swollen jaw or a nasty looking bruise somewhere on your body.

5.   A solid measure of skid marks left on the highway by the motor vehicle that smashed into you.

6.   Terrific gouges in the highway at the point of impact.

7.   Your missing a crucial business meeting, wedding, etc.

8.   School records indicating some serious problems developing because of your being absent from class.

9.   Dealing with so much discomfort you had no choice but to hire somebody (a relative is perfectly acceptable - just keep a record of the cancelled checks) to come into your home to perform some general housekeeping, or help to take care of your children, and/or cook the meals.

Any one of the above have the potential to increase one of the 4 "Values" **BASE** has provided for you. Put two or three of them together and there's little doubt you can elevate the settlement "Value" you originally thought you should be aiming for several notches higher to the next "Value."

There are *many* such items that can and will send shock waves penetrating into the area of how much a claim is worth. You should always feel comfortable deciding to go for a higher "Value," if your decision is based on *proof* that the settlement figure you've chosen to aim for is reasonable.

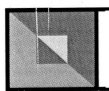
In order to effectively utilize **The BASE Formula**, we must separate Property Damage from Special Damages. To do this, we will place "Damages" into four categories.

The first two categories we will address are Property Damage and Compensatory Damage (defined as "Pain and Suffering").

The other two categories are what we will call **Special Damages.** These include Medical Special Damage Expenses and Non-Medical Special Damage Expenses.

## I. PROPERTY DAMAGE EXPENSES

These typically include:

1. Auto Repair

2. Vehicle Towing and Storage

3. Cost of Substitute Car Rental

4. Damaged Clothing, Watch, Jewelry, etc.

5. Broken Eye Glasses

## 2. COMPENSATORY DAMAGES

These are the dollars typically paid to the injured person for the "pain and suffering" they endured because of the bodily injury they received as a result of the accident they were in.

When using **The BASE Formula**, we will calculate the value of the Compensatory Damages by totaling the Special Damages and applying a factor to these Special Damages. A detailed listing of "Special Damages" follows.

It is important to understand the concept of "SPECIAL DAMAGES."

"Special Damages" include all costs other than Property Damage. These "Special Damages" costs are multiplied by a factor of up to 4 or even 5 when using **The BASE Formula** to determine the value of your claim including "pain and suffering" (see below and Chapter 8). Please review the following list carefully.

## 3. MEDICAL SPECIAL DAMAGE EXPENSES

1. Ambulance

2. Emergency Room Care

3. Hospital or Clinic

4. Doctor, Chiropractor, Specialist,

5 Over-the-counter Drugs and/or Prescription Medications

6. Laboratory Fees and Services

7. Diagnostic Tests: X-rays, (CT) Scan

8. Prosthetic Appliances or Surgical Apparatus (Canes and Crutches)

9. Physical Therapy

10. Registered and/or Practical Nurse

11. Ace Bandages

12. Gauze and Tape

13. Heating Pads

14. Creams, Lotions, Ointments, Balms

## 4. NON-MEDICAL SPECIAL DAMAGE EXPENSES

1. Lost Wages and Earnings

2. Lost Vacation Time and/or Sick Leave

3. Travel Expenses (transportation expenses incurred getting to and from the doctor and/or hospital)

4. Household Help During Disability

5. Child Care During Recuperation

40

## 5. LOST TIME AND EARNINGS

The days and hours you were unable to function at work, either full or part-time, thus the money you may have lost, is added up. This constitutes one of the most important elements of your "Non-Medical Special Damages," namely LOST WAGES. You shouldn't view your time away from work, because of an injury, as Lost Time and Earnings but rather as **Lost Earning Capacity**. *To implement BASE you must factor in your lost time and earnings, even if you've had no actual loss of money!* For example, when your salary is paid because you've taken sick leave, or because of an accident and health policy that's available to you, or some other similar arrangement, you've still accumulated a dollar figure that determines your Lost Earning capacity. That's the number you must use to properly calculate **BASE**.

### Documenting Lost Income

If you're employed by someone else, collecting information about your lost income is relatively simple. Ask your supervisor, boss, or the person in charge of such matters where you're employed, to write a letter for you on company stationary. This letter should include: your name, position, rate of pay, the number of hours you normally work, and the number of hours or days you missed because of the accident. (Review APPENDIX E: Sample Of Lost Wage and Earning Verification).

### You should also ask yourself these two questions:

1. Did the injury necessitate a change of job or employment?
2. Did the injury allow you to get back to work only part time?

If the answer to one or both of these two questions is "yes," ask your employer to document these facts on his letterhead. The proof of either should positively influence your decision to move *up* from one **BASE** "Value" to another.

### 5.1. If You're Employed Full Or Part Time

#### 5.1.1. <u>Full Time</u>

Be ready to discuss your job description and how long you've been employed at your current position:

1. Does your work demand heavy labor and/or lifting?

2. Did you lose any vacation time or sick leave?

3. Was there any loss of future earning capacity?

4. Where you absent from any important business meetings?

5.        Where you unable to make appointments with important or potential customers?

6.        Did you lose any bonuses?

7.        Did you miss the opportunity for an interview that might have led to a better job?

### 5.1.2. <u>Part Time</u>

If you were working relatively steady prior to the accident you shouldn't have any difficulty determining your lost wages for the period of time you lost. If your work was sporadic – sometimes earning a living wage, but at other times little or nothing - you can prove the value of your weekly lost earning capacity by providing the adjuster with your previous year's W2 and dividing that figure by 52.

## 5.2. If You're Self-Employed Or Own A Business

Be sure to add to the bottom line of **The BASE Value** you've elected to aim for, the cost of any additional help you had to hire while you were undergoing medical treatment or recuperating. To help prove your Lost Earning Capacity be ready to supply copies of your prior year's federal, and state, income tax returns. These may prove helpful for verification of the figures you arrived at. (See APPENDIX F:). Be ready to discuss the following.

1.        If your work demands heavy labor or lifting.

2.        How many hours you normally work each day. Each week.

3.        Your average income per week.

4.        Did your business lose money while you were laid up? Why? How much? Can you prove it?

To substantiate your loss you should consider presenting to the adjuster:

1.        Whatever documents will prove a loss in billing or invoices.

2.        A calendar showing appointments you had to cancel.

3.        Letters or documents proving business meeting you had to cancel.

## 5.3. Commissions And Overtime

Commissions and overtime can make a substantial difference in your lost earnings. If you were deprived of either they should be calculated as "lost earning capacity" when you implement **The BASE Formula**. Be sure to obtain a letter from your employer, on his letterhead, spelling out the approximate amount of money you lost in commissions and overtime. If your employer wonders how to do this, explain that it can be accomplished by reviewing last year's figures, for the same period, and then averaging them for the time you were unable to work because of the accident. By proceeding in that manner it should become a fairly simple task to compare your last year's figures against the earning time you lost because of the accident and come up with a number.

## 5.4. Tips And Gratuities

You may be employed where tips, such as waitress work, or gratuities, such as board and lodging, will make a difference in your lost earnings. Be sure to document these. Your employer can and should help you. Once you're fully recovered, ask him to state these facts on his letterhead.

## 5.5. If You're A Housewife

While it's extremely difficult to estimate a housewife's "lost earning capacity," it nevertheless must be done. In order to successfully execute **The BASE Formula** two basic questions that arise are, how does one determine what a housewife's wages should be? And also, how would one arrive at a *fair* figure? Before I answer that I would like to offer my sincere apologies to every at-home mom or housewife in America who reads this and considers hanging me in effigy. But, the only way this can be accomplished is to check, in your particular area, what the fair market value of a full-time domestic servant is. That is, one who doesn't live in. ("Live in" means provided room and board on the premises).

Find out what the hourly rate is and use that figure as a guideline. In this category, as in all others, both "full time" and "part time" lost earnings are involved. For example, if a housewife is totally disabled and confined to bed for two weeks, then her lost earning capacity is roughly that of a domestic servant's lost earnings for two weeks. If a housewife is only able to get up and around for half days then her lost earning capacity is roughly that of a domestic servant's half days of lost earnings. To help prove this it would be prudent for a housewife to keep a diary of how many hours of each day she was confined to bed, or to her living room couch, etc., and had no choice but to rest. Whatever figure a housewife comes up with should be factored into **The BASE Formula** in the area of Non-Medical Special Damage Expenses (Lost Wages). She should also include extraordinary expenses incurred because of her inability to perform certain tasks, such as gardening, car-pooling, etc.

## 5.6. Sick Leave Or Vacation Pay

At this point the fact that you were able to take sick leave or vacation pay during the period you missed from work, therefore not actually losing any income, must be touched upon. Keep in mind you would have been entitled to use that sick leave, or vacation time, for other times when you may have needed or wanted it. Using your sick leave, or your vacation pay, is to be considered *the same* as losing the pay itself!    Remember, when it comes to the issue of lost income, and the implementation of **The BASE Formula**, whether your lost wages were paid to you by some outside insurance coverage source, like sick leave, vacation pay, *or whatever*, to be reimbursed for lost income (your lost earning capacity) you need only prove (a) the time you missed from work because of the accident and (b) how much money you would have made during the period you missed.   The point is that you should calculate this into **The BASE Formula** *even if you were paid* in some other way.

## 5.7. Lost Opportunities

In addition to time lost from work, you're also entitled to be compensated for work opportunities you may not have been able to take advantage of because of your injuries. Proving a lost opportunity, such as a job interview or a scheduled sales meeting, which could add to the **BASE** "Value" you've decided to aim for, is much more difficult to prove than lost work hours.   But, even if you can't point to *specific* dollar amounts you may have lost, the fact is that the adjuster knows the potential, in the area of "lost opportunities" (situations you were unable to take advantage of) are legitimate issues and if somewhere down the line they were presented to a sympathetic judge or jury, they could indeed increase the dollar value of your claim.   As best you can, these figures should be presented to justify **The BASE Formula** "Value" you're aiming for. However, be sure to keep in mind that how much your settlement figure is increased will depend upon how legitimate your *proof* is of that lost income opportunity and how much money it might have cost you.

## 5.8. Your Age

The younger or older you are the better. Because of their obvious innocence, motor vehicle victims, between the ages of 1 and 12, generally have *outstanding* settlement results. On the other hand, because of their normally robust condition, and because they are generally at the height of their physical stamina, individuals between the ages of 21 and 59 aren't usually the recipients of unusual compassion in a court of law. Those in their late 60's, or over, generally fare *extremely* well. This is due to the sympathy often displayed by a judge or jury toward the elderly. Age should be considered when determining which of the four **BASE Values** you that you're going to aim for. (See CHAPTER 8).

## 5.9. Household Help, Child Care And Travel Costs

It doesn't matter if you're employed full-time, part-time, self-employed, own your own business, are retired, unemployed, or a housewife/mother not employed outside the home, you should document all household help, or child-care you had to hire during your period of disability, plus all unusual transportation costs (bus or taxi, etc.) incurred getting to and from the doctor, therapist, hospital, etc. These figures should be taken into consideration when you decide which "Value" to aim for.

## 5.10.  Gross Pay Vs Net Pay

You should factor into **BASE** the gross wages you lost, not the net. For every week of Total Disability (a fact your attending physician *must* state in the discharge medical report - see CHAPTER 6: YOUR BODILY INJURY) your doctor declares, you should use your *total* weekly income *before taxes*, even if you were paid. This is your "lost earning capacity" the concept, background, and information which was discussed earlier in this chapter.

For every week of Partial Disability stated in the medical report, you can claim up to 50% of your daily and/or weekly income, even if you didn't lose any. Whatever the situation may be, in order to implement **The BASE Formula**, you should always calculate and factor into **BASE** your *gross* income figure; *not your net!*

---

# IN SUMMARY REGARDING LOST WAGES

In order to properly apply **The BASE Formula** you must include the time you lost from work as a part of your claim or you will not be maximizing your claim value. As stated above, you can claim this "lost earning potential" even if you were paid during this period whether through sick leave, regular pay or otherwise.

---

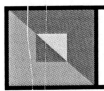
Rules for evaluating the property damage to a motor vehicle are fairly straightforward. In general, when the repair costs for the vehicle are less than the vehicle's market value (i.e. your damaged vehicle is not completely wrecked and can still be repaired), your reimbursement for the damage will be equal to what it will cost to repair it. But where, on the other hand, your repair costs *exceed* the vehicle's "fair market value," your reimbursement will be equal to only the fair market value of the vehicle

Insurance adjusters use a number of published guidebooks as their primary tool to determine the actual cash value of a motor vehicle. One of the oldest guides used is the "Kelly Blue Book." It's available at your local public library and on the internet.

## I. WHAT DOES (ACV) ACTUAL CASH VALUE MEAN?

Basically, this is the replacement cost of an item *less* depreciation. It's the amount you would have to pay to replace your motor vehicle, with a similar model in similar condition. When it's destroyed you're not paid what it originally cost but rather, the actual cash value (ACV). Mileage, accessories, condition of tires, etc. are all taken into consideration.

## 2. SOME GENERAL CONSIDERATIONS

If an insurance adjuster is not going to make a payment, after the investigation has been completed and the exact amount of the property damage has been determined, he should decline payment promptly. If a payment is going to be made, he evaluates it by checking the bills carefully. The following are examples of what he looks for:

1.  Replacement of parts that were not damaged by the accident

2.  Replacement of parts where the damage was caused by ordinary wear and tear

3.  Charges made for new parts, although used parts were installed

4.  Overcharge on parts

5.  Duplication of parts and labor items

6.     Inclusion of previous damage into the new damage estimate

7.     Incorrect addition

## 3.  TOTAL LOSS

In the evaluation of a total loss, it's important to know what the general condition of the car was before the accident and mileage on the odometer is checked.   If the car is so badly damaged that it cannot be driven, you don't have to obtain more than one written estimate - although the insurance company will probably want to have one of its own inspectors take a look at it to determine if indeed it *was* totaled. "Totaled" doesn't necessarily mean that the vehicle can't be fixed, but that the repairs would cost more than it's worth. If that's the case, the insurance company will only pay you the motor vehicle's actual cash value (ACV).

They will not pay to have the vehicle repaired. The car's ACV is determined by comparing it with the current sale price, in your particular area of the country, of a similar year, make and model.

The figures arrived at by using this guide are not absolute. If the price that's stated in the guide seems too low, you may refuse to accept it. It's perfectly legitimate to insist that the guidebook figure be averaged out with the prices of identical vehicles currently being sold on the local used car lots, or as advertised in your local newspaper's classified adds.

The figures that these guides/tables indicate are not set in cement. There's no law that requires you to accept the figures, as stated.  In a property damage settlement, depreciated values are reached by using common sense, negotiation, and mutual agreement. You shouldn't permit an adjuster to force you into accepting his value of an item "because that's what the book says it's worth." What's important, in obtaining an equitable settlement, is to determine what it would cost you to duplicate, as nearly as possible, the property that's been destroyed. However, you must take into consideration, the age and the amount of use that vehicle has been subjected to.

If you feel you're not being treated fairly don't be hesitant to bargain, dicker, or argue with the adjuster about the value of your motor vehicle, or any other personal property that was damaged. It's *your* money!

## 4.  DEPRECIATION

This is the amount of wear and tear on an item. Depreciation should be based on a standard guide.  Ask the adjuster to provide you with the source of his depreciation figure.

48

## 5. FAIR MARKET VALUE

This is the value of your vehicle with consideration shown for the year, make, model options, mileage, and the general condition of your vehicle and its components (i.e. tires, interior, paint, etc.).

## 6. OTHER PROPERTY DAMAGE

If someone is liable to you for your personal injuries they're also responsible for any damage they may have caused to your personal property. Such property damage can occur to clothes, eye glasses, a watch and/or jewelry, etc. In other words, any object you happen to be carrying on your person, or in your motor vehicle, that was damaged or destroyed. To expect recovery you must be able to visibly present to the adjuster the property that was damaged. Then, you must prove its value in writing from whomever it was purchased. Also, if possible, request that the document states the date you purchased it.

You should make copies of all bills relating to these damages. Be sure to have these documents in your possession when you and the adjuster sit down to talk. Photocopies are acceptable to give to him.

---

## TWO CRUCIAL PROPERTY DAMAGE REMINDERS

1.  Double-check your check.   Read the fine print.

    Once you accept a property damage settlement, you're forever prevented from claiming there's still more damage to your motor vehicle.

    Carefully review your property damage settlement check, and any accompanying "Release":

    a.  Make sure it's written as "Property Damage Only."

    b.  Don't deposit a check or sign a release saying "General Release."

    c.  Insist the adjuster indicates "Property Damage Only" on a check.

2.  Any charges you may have incurred for towing, storage, substitute car rental, or alternate transportation, are legitimate out-of-pocket expenses you should be reimbursed for. Make sure you provide the adjuster with copies of all paid receipts.

49

| | |
|---|---|
| # Your Bodily Injury | Auto Accident Personal Injury Insurance Claim |
| | **CHAPTER 6** |
| | © 2002 Daniel G. Baldyga |

Note: This is a very long chapter that covers a great deal of ground in regards to various types of injuries. It is not necessary that you read and fully understand all aspects of this section (arthritis, etc.) if they do not apply to your situation.

## I. WHAT DOES THE INJURY MEAN TO YOU?

It will mean personal out-of-pocket expenses that include the cost of repairing your motor vehicle and medical bills. More often than not there will be a period of time that you're unable to work, resulting in lost wages, a sudden shock to your lifestyle and a tremendous inconvenience. There will likely be either a short or prolonged period of pain that you will suffer because of your injury. All of these are the direct result of a motor vehicle accident that wasn't your fault. The *only* way you can be compensated for this is by receiving money – a financial reward! This payment should include property damage, medical bills, the total of your other out-of-pocket expenses, *plus* an additional amount of money for your "pain and suffering" (your "Compensatory Damages") to be paid to you because of all you were subjected to.

A small percentage of auto accidents are responsible for serious injuries. If your medical diagnosis includes bone fractures, a herniated disk, serious aggravation of a pre-existing condition, prenatal difficulties, almost anything diagnosed to be more complicated than a "Soft Tissue" type of injury, then it's not wise for you to attempt to handle your claim yourself. You should engage an attorney to represent you.

### THE HIGHER THE MEDICAL BILLS THE HIGHER THE SETTLEMENT VALUE OF YOUR CLAIM

The ultimate value of a personal injury claim has a direct relationship to the amount of your medical bills. Why? Because a claim with doctors bills of $500.00 is worth three to five times more than a claim with bills of $100.00. The adjuster will reason if you were hurt badly enough to generate medical expenses of $500.00, or more, then your injuries must have been fairly substantial. But, if you see a doctor once and your bills are less than $100.00, the adjuster will assume you weren't hurt too seriously. It's a fundamental fact of insurance claim settlement negotiations that the more doctor visits you make, the higher the medical bills will be, and therefore the greater value your claim will have. That's the reason you should provide yourself with all necessary medical treatment, and as often as recommended.

51        © 1999-2003 Daniel G. Baldyga

## YOU MUST BE EXAMINED BY YOUR DOCTOR OR YOUR CHIRO-PRACTOR AS SOON AS POSSIBLE.

It is an indispensable necessity that you see a doctor or chiropractor to get medical attention as quickly as possible after an accident. This decision can often make the difference between ending up with a fistful of hundred dollar bills for your loss, or a paltry "nuisance value" settlement (a small payment made by the insurance company) to close the case.

If you don't see a doctor or chiropractor, but still attempt to justify an injury that produced "pain and discomfort", and you also contend to have lost time from work, the adjuster will not buy it. At the end of the day you won't be paid much for your loss. But if you do see a doctor, and after they have discharged you with a respectable Medical Report, the settlement value of your case improves tremendously.

> Your claim of bodily injury has no credibility with the Insurance Adjuster unless it has been verified by the Medical Report of your attending physician

## 2. SIGNS AND SYMPTOMS

Doctors are very specific when they use certain terms to describe findings in their medical report and they often make a distinction between "signs" and "symptoms."

**SIGNS:** A sign is something that can be physically documented by the physician or chiropractor. A fracture seen on the x-ray, a black-and-blue bruise that can be photographed, or a cut which required stitches and will leave a permanent scar .

**SYMPTOMS:** The symptom of an injury is a more subtle, subjective finding. It cannot be documented by physical findings that are easy to demonstrate or reproduce reliably on paper. You cannot measure it or photograph it. Symptoms can be such things as fatigue due to stress, neck soreness due to whiplash, or tingling fingers due to cervical spine nerve root inflammation. This doesn't mean these aren't true and important problems but only that modern medical science has yet to develop the technology to concretely document these findings for the medical record.

It's important that your doctor document both Signs and Symptoms, which are a direct result of your accident, so there's a full and accurate description of your injuries.

## IF YOUR INJURY IS RELATIVELY MILD

Under normal, routine circumstances your doctor will probably, on the average, see you three to six times (occasionally more) without providing you with any complicated treatment.

You can expect, in this typical situation, to be x-rayed, prescribed some pills, told to rest a few days or weeks, and possibly be advised to avail yourself of heat therapy, to be administered at home.

## IF YOUR INJURY IS MORE SERIOUS

You may have to wear a cervical collar (a neck brace) for a few weeks. This can be uncomfortable but it will assist in your physical recovery and most assuredly produce a higher settlement value of your claim. Your doctor may also refer you to a specialist, such as an orthopedist (bone doctor) or a neurologist (specialist in nerve disorders). If you have a very serious injury, it is suggested that you contact an attorney. This book is primarily intended for those who are involved in an accident with a clear case of liability and no serious injuries.

## 3. TYPES OF INJURIES

For purposes of evaluation we'll divide injuries into two general categories:

### 3.1. Soft Tissue Injuries

The major evidence of these types of injuries is the description of the discomfort the patient experienced. This is learned from the doctor's Medical Report. For example, a sprained neck, ankle or back is a Soft Tissue injury. What are involved are muscles and other connective tissue. These types of aches and pains make up the vast majority of motor vehicle accident injuries. They're the kind of discomforts you'll have to live with for awhile. But you don't need outside help to successfully settle your claim if you have these kinds of injuries. Certainly not in a case where the liability is clearly the fault of the person who struck you. What you do need is thorough and detailed documentation from your attending physician.

### 3.2. Hard Injuries

These are injuries that can be specifically observed through medical examination, such as broken bones, ligament or cartilage damage, a spinal disk rupture or vertebra dislocation. Motor vehicle bodily injury situations like these make up a very small percentage of insurance claims. When one has to deal with these types of medical problems it's best to obtain competent legal assistance.

# BASIC BACKGROUND INJURY INFORMATION

*The Following Should Not Be Misconstrued Or Interpreted As Comprehensive Medical Facts, But Only As Basic Background Regarding Injuries As They Fall Within The Framework Of A General Discussion Of Insurance Claims.*

## 4. MINOR BODILY INJURIES

The vast majority of auto accidents cause minor injuries. While bodily injury pain can be specifically measured (temperament and psychological factors are deeply involved), the limits of human endurance cannot. Each individual has a different "pain threshold," identified as the point at which one begins to feel physical pain. The amount and quality of pain you feel is not strictly dependent on the bodily injury inflicted. It has much to do with your previous experiences, how well you remember them, and your ability to understand the cause of the pain and its consequences. For example, the ex-hockey player will probably experience a blow much differently than the individual who never played contact sports.

## 5. HOW MUCH PAIN CAN A PERSON STAND?

There's no specific answer to that question. Sudden pain, even of less intensity than, for example, a serious burn, can still overwhelm the higher nerve centers; so much so that one may fall into a faint.

## 6. NERVE IMPULSES

Suppose you touch a hot stove. The intense heat with which your finger has come into contact is converted to a code of electrical nerve signals. This takes place in tiny nerve endings in the skin called pain receptors. These receptors are busy networks of fibers with broad and overlapping, highly sensitive fields. Each network transmits its own coded pattern of nerve impulses to the brain.

## 7. SPINAL CORD

In the spinal cord, the relays of pain receptor fibers connect with certain nerve fibers that run from the memory-storing area of the brain. These fibers serve to interpret the original message picked up by the pain receptors. They're the means by which memories of past experiences can intensify, or minimize, pain. A sharp blow to the ribs of a woman who played varsity sports may not be felt nearly so acutely as it would to a woman of the same size, weight, and height who spends her leisure hours collecting stamps, chasing butterflies or watching birds.

54

## 8. STRAIN AND STRESS

It's also known that stress and strain aggravate physical pain. When you're under severe psychological stress, it may be magnified to the point where the only relief is a drug. It's a realistic premise that someone who has just been in an auto accident will have a greater degree of headache pain than he or she will have, from the same kind of headache, when experienced under less severe circumstances such as, for example, while gathered around a piano singing Christmas carols with their loved ones.

## 9. ANXIETY

Anxiety can greatly increase pain. When you expect an experience to be painful, your "pain threshold" will decrease. If your last trip to the dentist was pleasant, when you next visit him your anxiety level will probably not be nearly as high as if, during your previous session, you experienced excruciating pain.

## 10. EMOTIONAL REACTIONS

There are also emotional reactions to the injury. A bodily injury is bound to cause some degree of emotional imbalance. The duration and severity of that reaction depends upon a combination of factors:

1. The type of individual you are.

2. The severity and health consequences of the injury you sustained.

3. The life stress, or strengths, you're experiencing at the time of your injury.

A woman who is by nature a "shrinking violet," and in the midst of a professional crisis or a grueling divorce, is going to react differently to her accident injury than a woman of the same age and background who has a strong self-image and has recently received an award for her accomplishments.

## 11. MUSCLES

You're struck a mighty blow in the rear of your automobile. Sudden movements will affect your body as it's whipped and bounced around inside your car and can cause the many muscles in your neck, back, buttocks, arms, legs, and thighs to be injured, generating pain, from mild to severe. A muscle bruised or torn to the point of bleeding can cause what's known as the extremely painful "charlie horse." With the

55

proper medical guidance, an injured muscle can be treated and healed. When it comes to muscle injuries something to keep in mind is that when one portion of the body demands rest (by sending out a pain signal) you unconsciously help your body by placing a new burden on another set of muscles.

Although these muscles may not have been directly injured in the accident they are nevertheless undergoing stress because of their new role. You can begin to experience pain in a healthy and uninjured part of your body as your body mechanics cause you to misuse other muscles in order to protect the muscles injured in the accident. For example: If you injured your left hip in an accident, and can't support your weight on your left leg properly, you'll try to put an unusual amount of weight on your right hip and leg, in order to ambulate and get around. By the end of the day, you may find that your right hip is very sore, and not understand why. That's because you're actually causing the right hip to become painfully strained, as a result of your altered body mechanics.

In some cases, you can aggravate dormant arthritis, or an old injury. This then becomes a secondary result of the accident, due to this compensatory response to your injuries. It's important that you make use of any necessary supportive walking devices, such as a cane or crutch, as directed by your physician or chiropractor.

## 12. REFERRED PAIN

It's possible to experience pain in an area of the body that wasn't injured in the automobile accident but is, in fact, a direct result of the event. This is identified as Referred Pain. Here's how it works:

Nerves carry pain messages from your extremities to your brain, by way of your spinal cord. If you injure your nerve, higher up along the pathway, you may experience the pain as generating from lower in the pathway.

For example: Say you have a pinched nerve in your neck. This nerve usually carries impulses from your fingers to your brain. You may suddenly discover that your fingers are tingly or numb, and you can't write properly or tie your shoes. You're perplexed, because you know your hand was not injured. However, the problem is that the nerve in your neck is experiencing swelling around it, caused by the inflammation from the neck injury. It's almost as if the nerve is confused. It only knows how to explain it to you by way of its normal sensory distribution. In that particular situation your numb fingers are actually a "referred" pain from your neck injury.

## 13. TENDONS AND LIGAMENTS

Twisted, bruised, battered, pulled and snapped tendons and ligaments are often the results of a motor vehicle accident.

### TENDON
A tendon is a band of strong tissue which connects muscle to bone. It can be torn where it's attached to either the muscle or the bone, and can cause a great deal of pain, due to the inflammation the body causes while it's trying to repair itself. One of the most famous tendons is the "Achilles Tendon," which attaches at the back of the heel. (So named because it's where Achilles' mother held him when she dipped him into the liquid which made him invincible, except for the spot where she was holding him, therefore he was only vulnerable there, at his "Achilles Tendon").

### LIGAMENT
A ligament is also a band of strong tissue, but it specifically connects bone to bone. Injuries which cause strong shearing forces can separate a ligament from its bony attachment, causing severe pain, due to inflammation, and possible local bleeding at the site of the injury.

## 14. ATROPHY

The prolonged non-use of a muscle will cause it to shrink. When this occurs it's called atrophy. The human body, with its fantastic ability to rebuild, will bring that muscle back to normal a short time after you begin to use it again.

## 15. SCARS

It's not easy to evaluate the physical and unique damages of a scar. If the cut is straight and the edges are brought together, there may be a line for awhile but at the end of perhaps six months to a year the color will probably disappear and the scar won't be noticeable. Jagged scars, however, can cause contraction of the muscles and may always remain visible. Scars on the normally visible parts of the body of a man or woman whose physical appearance is of paramount importance in their work, models for example, will certainly have much more value than scars that might be visible on the arms or legs of a construction laborer whose work depends little on a flawless physical appearance.

Besides photographs another method of helping to explain a scarring of the face is to clip out facial pictures from print advertisements. These will provide good background on which to draw a scar so as to demonstrate the location and extent of the scar.

57

## 16. JOINTS

The most drastic disability results from simple dislocation of moveable joints. Moveable joints include the ball and socket joint, which finds the round head of one bone fitting into a cup-like cavity of another, as in the shoulder, the hip, and the gliding joint of the wrist and ankle. The following are some of the various medical problems which can become a reality as a result of a joint injury:

1. A bone becomes separated from its socket.

2. Muscles are pulled from their attachments.

3. Tendons and ligaments are torn or stretched.

4. Cartilage is found to be floating freely outside their bearing joints.

Under enough force, practically every joint in the body can be dislocated. Often forces that work toward dislocation merely stretch ligaments, causing sprains. Sometimes the ligaments are pulled or frayed or even wrenched from their bindings at the joint. The most common sprains afflict fingers, wrist, knee and ankle.

## 17. ARTHRITIS

A major affliction of the joints is arthritis. It's the most widespread chronic body affliction and the number-one crippling disease in the United States. Nearly everyone over the age of 50 has the potential for some degree of arthritis. A severe blow to a joint can either aggravate or bring on the arthritic condition at the point of the blow. Arthritis is a condition that can lay dormant or undetected until your accident. It is perhaps the insurance claim industry's number one vexation. A good rule of thumb to keep in mind regarding arthritic aggravation from a direct blow is as follows:

It's generally considered that if arthritic pain is triggered it should appear within a reasonably short time. Some medical books contend that a "reasonably short time" is within a week after impact. But the claims industry usually takes the position if it doesn't rear its ugly head in 24 to 48 hours after impact then the industry is loath to consider so-called arthritic pain to be anything more than just "old age creeping in."

Under normal conditions, in an attempt to declare a relationship between the accident and arthritic pain as part of your claim, three factors, which the adjuster knows are of paramount importance, come into play. These are as follow:

1. How hard a blow did you sustain?

2.     Did the blow take place in the area of your body where you're now experiencing arthritic pain?

3.     How long after the accident was it that the arthritic pain began?

If a long, pain free interval did exist, the only conclusion the adjuster can come to is that the arthritis is probably not related to the accident.


## 18. X-RAY EXAMINATIONS

In the absence of broken bones, the results of an x-ray examination can be highly questionable. Because it's almost impossible to determine what's normal, and what's not normal, in cases involving cervical spine or lower back injury, the x-ray report should never be the sole basis for any claims settlement. Other clinical information is essential. Your doctor knows this and he should provide you with it, in his written report of your physical condition, following the accident. The sooner after the accident you're medically evaluated and x-rayed, the more valid the medical reports will be to the adjuster assigned to handle your claim. Emotional tension can also produce spasms in various parts of your body, including the neck. That's why an accurate diagnosis of "whiplash" injury is almost impossible to make.


## 19. WHIPLASH

One of the most difficult injuries to diagnose is a condition called "whiplash," which means the backward and forward snapping of an individual's head, caused by the sudden acceleration and deceleration of a motor vehicle that has sustained a solid impact. Such a whipping around of ones body results in the stretching of neck muscles and/or ligaments that often produce muscle spasms.

Whiplash is a convenient way of designating certain "Accident Facts" that produce injury in the spinal cervical area. *The term carries no medical connotation that would properly bring it within the area of a medical diagnosis.* A whiplash-type injury can be very painful, however, and it can last a long time.

Without question, there are often, sometimes severe, injuries involving the cervical region of the spine. But, with the misuse of the term whiplash, it automatically makes those in the business of settling personal injury claims highly suspicious. To many of them the term "whiplash" is a medical smokescreen, described as such to confuse, delude and defraud.

When it comes time to settle your case you, as the recipient of a legitimate whiplash-type injury, must be in a position to emphatically stress (and make sure your attending physician makes it clear in his medical report) that your whiplash is authentic.

59

## How Whiplash Happens

An individual sitting in a car seat, especially with the head unsupported, upon receiving an unexpected impact in the rear, is subjected to a tremendous hyperextension force which, as has been shown in engineering studies and slow-motion pictures produced under test conditions, to be considerably more than the average person would expect. This phenomenon is said to be due to the unique anatomy of the neck (the top portion of the spine or Cervical Spine) in comparison to that of the rest of the vertebral column (the Thoracic-Lumbar Spine).

*Top of the spine neck*

## A Painful Experience

The suffering caused by a whiplash-type injury comes from the muscular strain, the stretching or tearing of tendons and ligaments and compression effects upon the arteries, nerves and nerve roots. (Fractures, dislocations, scar tissue, and actual disc damage are rarely encountered). In every instance the degree, depth and length of injury, plus the pain generated, can only be determined by the proper medical diagnosis of your doctor or chiropractor. Don't allow them to simply state in your written medical report, the word "whiplash," and let it go at that. If they don't go into detail it can be, and often is, the kiss of death at settlement time.

## The Symptoms

Beginning with the highest frequency the most common symptoms of a whiplash-type injury are as follows:

1.  Neck Pain: If related to the accident, this should appear within a few hours of injury, if not immediately.

2.  Neck Stiffness: A frequent symptom. It may derive from muscle spasm due to muscular injury. Most patients with this symptom also complain of a headache.

3.  Dizziness: A feeling of unsteadiness at intervals, indicating there's probably a momentary disruption of circulation to the brain.

4.  Other Discomforts: Some patients complain of distress in the shoulders, or down their arms and legs, with possible associated complaints of disturbances of sensation.

## Prognosis

With the right medical treatment (temporary splinting by means of a neck collar, accompanied by heat, and/or massage, and/or medication) one should expect steady improvement after the first two or three weeks. It's not unusual for total recovery to take three or four months. You *must* make sure your doctor or chiropractor's final Medical Report goes into the specifics of exactly how acute and painful your whiplash-type injury was, and why. You have every right to expect your doctors, upon discharge from their care, to provide you with a medical report which details your whiplash-type injury.

## 20. DOCUMENTING DISABILITY

The doctors' Medical Report must contain their comments regarding the nature of your disability. Their diagnosis is of monumental importance to the value of your claim because it reflects the duration and depth of your "pain and suffering." *It also proves that the time you lost from work is legitimate.*

At settlement time the adjuster will form a healthy portion of his evaluation based on the Medical Report which should clearly state the length of time of the two elements: **TOTAL DISABILITY** and **PARTIAL DISABILITY**. The best judge of your "total disability" and your "partial disability" is your attending physician. What he states in his report will prove the extent to which you were restricted from returning to work and also from participating in your normal, routine, social activities.

### Your Doctor Or Chiropractor's Role

Other than the usual, routine procedures your doctor or chiropractor will normally conduct to assist you in your recovery, and at the expense of being unnecessarily repetitive, it cannot be stressed enough that the written Medical Report they will eventually produce for you must be authoritative and decisive. If they don't provide specific detail, regarding your whiplash-type injury, they're not doing the right thing by you.

If you're examined a few days after the accident there will be some objective findings. These will consist of muscle spasms and limited neck motion. (X-rays will indicate nothing abnormal since the damages are soft tissue which don't show up on x-rays). Be sure that the Medical Record details any limitations in your range of motion, or strength.

In an overwhelming majority of cases the problems from a whiplash-type injury tend to resolve themselves in a period of convalescence. If arthritis is present in the spine at the time of such an injury, your doctor must make it clear in their Medical Report. If indeed arthritis is involved one can expect a much longer period of time needed to fully recover.

61

## 21. TOTAL DISABILITY AND PARTIAL DISABILITY

There are many conceptions of so-called total and partial disabilities. Views differ between insurance companies, lawyers, and doctors. In most cases the term boils down to unofficial, personal, concepts. The doctor's evaluation is the most qualified.

**TOTAL DISABILITY:** Total disability is that period of time you're unable to perform your normal work, your social commitments and your Activities Of Daily Living , often identified as ADL by attending physicians. It's that period of time you're confined to your home and can only leave your bed or couch to visit your doctor.

**PARTIAL DISABILITY:** Partial disability is that period of time you are greatly limited in work and social commitments. A time when you're barely able to struggle through your usual day's labor, both at home or at work, and at much less than your normal capacity and efficiency. To be considered to be in a state of partial disability, you must still be under your doctor's care and making office visits at close intervals.

## 22. WHAT A MEDICAL REPORT SHOULD CONTAIN

Your Medical Report should contain the following in as much detail as possible.

1.  Is your disability solely a result of the accident? If "no," explain.

2.  Are there any pre-existing conditions or factors which were aggravated by your injuries? If so, explain.

3.  What treatments were administered?   Why and for what duration?

4.  What over-the-counter and prescription medications were prescribed? In what amounts and for how long? What symptoms or medical problems were such medications meant to relieve?  Describe any adverse reactions.

5.  In the doctor's opinion, what is the nature, extent and frequency of the pain that an injury, such as yours, will likely cause?

6.  PROGNOSIS: Information on your progress. What part was played by a pre-existing condition, if any? Prediction of temporary or total disability impairments? Is it anticipated that there may be further treatments?

7.  Your TOTAL Disability: Stated in weeks and days. When ended?

8.  Your PARTIAL Disability: Stated in weeks and days. When ended?

9.  Did the accident cause any injury which is likely to "flare" in the future, with only the slightest provocation?

62

To provide yourself with the ammunition and the ability to put together an in-depth presentation, one which will help you to determine the "Value" you've decided to aim for, *plus* furnish the adjuster with your justification for being paid that particular "Value," see APPENDIX G: Personal Injury Damages Checklist.

## 23. SUBJECTIVE COMPLAINTS

Subjective complaints are extremely important in evaluating your disability. Subjective means these complaints are felt and described by you but are impossible to measure in an objective manner. Complaints, such as pain, numbness, weakness, fatigue, and tenderness in a particular area, are among the most common.

Since there is little in the way of an objective measurement of a subjective complaint, your doctor should report all of them in detail, including duration, frequency, location, severity, and the manner of interference they caused in normal use, and also in your occupation, along with a detailed evaluation of them.

Be sure to report *all* your complaints to your doctor. With their knowledge of anatomy, physiology, and the mechanics of the body, they're in the best position to judge whether such complaints are injury related, reasonable and physical in nature. Be sure that you inform your doctor or chiropractor about any non-prescription medication you're using to relieve your pain. This information should be in their report.

## 24. THE "SENIOR CITIZEN" CRASH VICTIM

With the average individual life span increasing, the population beyond the ages of 60 continues to grow. This expanding segment of the population is prone to injury, especially the kind that results from the impact of one motor vehicle smashing into another. If you're an older motor vehicle crash victim your doctor should take this into consideration in their written evaluation of your condition.

## 25. OTHER MEDICAL REPORT CONSIDERATIONS

It's not uncommon for people to be reluctant to reveal to their attending physician information about pre-existing conditions. They very often forget facts regarding their medical history. Many times people will insist they attained full recovery from a specific health problem that occurred in the past, and any current disability or discomfort is not related to that past event. Or, they may honestly feel that what they're experiencing is pain from previous symptoms and disabilities aggravated by the current accident. Whatever the case may be, your doctor, in his written report, must be careful to draw these distinctions.

You'll need the doctor's detailed report to properly evaluate your claim. It's not unreasonable for him to charge you for this report. If necessary, make a trip to his office and personally ask for it. You have every right to obtain it. They know the medical facts are extremely important, both to you and to the adjuster .

**BECAUSE IT'S SO CRUCIAL, AND AT THE RISK OF BEING UNDULY REPETITIVE, IT MUST BE STATED AGAIN:**

In order for you, and the adjuster, to discuss and properly evaluate your injury, the Medical Report should be detailed, and clearly state, in the four following areas:

1. Length of partial disability.

2. Length of total disability.

3. Your inability to perform certain functions.

4. The existence or probability of permanent or disabling effects.

Doctors are familiar with the accident claim process and will understand what you're requesting and why. Never forget, it's your right to obtain a Medical Report from your attending physician. Make sure the report comes to you and not the adjuster. This way, you'll have the opportunity to review its contents. If it's a fair and accurate report, you can, when the time is ripe, mail or hand a copy to the adjuster. If it's not a fair or complete report, you remain in a position to call the doctor's attention to any inaccuracies or omissions and ask for a revision before you submit it to the adjuster. If, after reading the Medical Report, you discover the doctor or chiropractor hasn't included their estimate of the *length of time* of your TOTAL DISABILITY or your PARTIAL DISABILITY (it happens) *go back and ask him to state it* !

## 26. HOSPITAL RECORDS AND REPORTS

If you were there, the hospital will have records of your treatment. Whether you were an in-patient, or an out-patient in the emergency room, you're entitled to copies of all examination records, including x-ray and CT scan. Get them. Be sure to secure copies of all medical bills that the hospital has on record.

## 27. YOUR "PAIN AND SUFFERING"  (Compensatory Damages)

The type of injury you suffered, as a result of your motor vehicle accident, plus the nature and duration of your treatment, are the two basic indicators of the degree of "pain and suffering" you experienced. However, there are several other areas you can point out to the adjuster to make him aware of the ongoing trauma you endured. These are as follow:

**MEDICATION:** The fact that you were prescribed either over-the-counter or prescription medication to relieve pain, inflammation, or any other injury symptoms, should help to convince the adjuster that your injuries were serious and they caused you to suffer. The stronger the medication and the longer prescribed, the greater its influence on the value of your claim.

**LENGTH OF RECOVERY:** The longer your recovery period, the greater your "pain and suffering," therefore the higher the settlement value your bodily injury claim will be. Make sure your attending physician notes this in their final report. Ask them to mention, in weeks and months, how long it should be, before you engage in certain activities.

As long as you continue to have physical problems you should keep going back to see your doctor, *again and again*. Other than the obvious ones there are two other very good reasons why:

1. The fact that your records show a visit to your doctor, four, six, eight (or even more) weeks after the accident, clearly indicates to the adjuster that your injury required continual attention.

2. When you visit your doctor, should it be true, be sure to tell him there has been little if any decrease of your pain, discomfort, stiffness or immobility. These continuing problems must be noted in their final report.

## 28. RESIDUAL OR PERMANENT INJURY

The simple and obvious reason that even a relatively small residual disability, or disfigurement, can greatly increase your award is that you'll suffer from it over a long period of time - perhaps *forever!* The more serious the effect on your life at work, home or recreation, the higher the value of your claim. If you've suffered an injury which is likely to be permanent - a limp, a bad back, or other such complications - you should seek representation by an experienced and competent attorney.

**SCARS:** Large and obvious scaring expands the value of your claim - especially if the scarred part of your body is normally visible. Take photographs! If the scar is bad enough ask your doctor to refer you to a plastic surgeon for an opinion as to whether your scar can be repaired or removed. Once examined, ask that specialist to detail in writing how much such a procedure would cost. Include the plastic surgeon's report, plus the bills for the visits to their office, etc., as part of your claim to the adjuster.

## 29. EMOTIONAL DISTRESS

Emotional difficulties should be compensated. They can cause stress, embarrassment, depression or strains on family relationships. For example the inability to take care of children, anxiety over the effects of an accident on your work or business, or interference with sexual relations. The most effective way to demonstrate that you've suffered emotional distress is to report it to your doctor. He should make note of your problems in his medical report. Insurance adjusters will accept that which appears in a Medical Record much quicker than what you report to them verbally. If your emotional distress is serious enough you should seek assistance from someone other than the physician treating your original injury. For example, a dietician for eating problems, a psychologist or some other therapist to cope with stress, or perhaps a marriage counselor because of problems that may have developed in your sexual relations. Charges for these expenses become a part of your damages and add value to your claim. The records of the specialist will serve as proof of any emotional problem you've been experiencing and dealing with.

## 30. SECURING COMPENSATION FOR LIFE DISRUPTIONS

If your injuries have caused you to miss school, or some other special training, you may want to make that time up. Your difficulty in making up that missed time (perhaps you had to give up a number of evenings and/or weekends to catch up and it can *never* be made up) has the potential to significantly increase the value of your settlement. Remember to obtain written proof.

## 31. MISSED VACATION OR RECREATION

If, because of your injuries, you were forced to give up your regular recreational activities for an extended period of time, or if your injuries caused you to cancel a vacation, family visit, or other trip or event, you're entitled to extra compensation. For example, if you're a runner or a hiker who has been unable to exercise, or someone who regularly participates in some area of physical training classes or activities, but were unable to do so for some time after the accident, you're entitled to be compensated for that loss. Document these lost activities as best you can.

## 32. CANCELLED SPECIAL EVENT

If your injuries made it impossible for you to attend an important or meaningful event such as a wedding, funeral, graduation, conference or reunion, etc., you are entitled to be compensated for that loss. To have one of these particular claims taken seriously you must prove it was a one time event which cannot be repeated.

66

## I. WHO THEY ARE AND HOW THEY WORK

Insurance adjusters come with different titles, such as claims specialist, claims representative or independent claims analyst. They have many titles but they usually have the same job, perform an equal function and do the same work. Understanding who claims adjusters are, and how they operate, should allow you to conclude they have no real advantage over you.

By having a solid understanding of the issues, as they apply to the typical motor vehicle accident claim, *plus* the knowledge of how to execute **BASE**, you'll level the playing field inside the arena where the two of you are jousting. When you've filed a claim against the person who was responsible for your damages the negotiation process will normally proceed to be dealt with by a claims adjuster for that individual's liability insurance company.

Occasionally, a claim is not assigned to an insurance company's salaried adjuster, but instead it's referred to a firm of independent adjusters. Insurance companies often do this if they don't have a local claims office in a particular area. Independent insurance adjusters representing an insurance company tend to operate in approximately the same manner as any in-house, company claims adjuster.

The only real difference is that they often have little, if any, dollar authority to settle a case. This means they must have your settlement amount approved by a claims supervisor, operating inside the insurance company which hired them to handle your case. The negotiation process itself, however, is routinely identical.

Public entities, such as governments or large cities, often have their own claims adjustment office. The negotiation process with these government adjusters usually functions the same as it does with company adjusters. The only notable difference in negotiating with a government claims adjuster is that if your claim ends up in court, judges and juries have a history of not being overly generous when awarding damages with the public's money. Knowing this ahead of time, government adjusters are tighter with settlement dollars than company adjusters.

Self-insured corporations, and some insurance companies who do not have a local claims office, will sometimes use their staff attorney, or a local lawyer, as their claims representative. Government entities sometimes have assistant city, county or state attorneys who handle accident claims.

67

© 1999-2003 Daniel G. Baldyga

Don't become alarmed should you discover a lawyer is handling your loss instead of an adjuster. When it comes to the claims negotiation process itself, a lawyer can't do anything different than a non-attorney claims adjuster.

It's a matter of record that an attorney handling a claim will often be easier to deal with than a company employed claims adjuster. This is because most lawyers realize that in smaller cases it's much better for the company to settle promptly rather than spending an excessive amount of time, which translates into a ton of money being spent. Lawyers don't work for minimum wages, trying to settle for a little less.

## 2. MOST CLAIMS ADJUSTERS ARE REASONABLY FAIR

Claims adjusters will usually deal fairly with you when you can *document* and *justify* your damages. If you display a knowledge and understanding of claims negotiation skills, comprehend the basic inner workings of the insurance claims process, *plus* have a good idea what your "pain and suffering" is worth, then chances are you're probably going to be treated fairly. In the majority of instances you'll most likely arrive at a reasonable settlement. Most claims adjusters aren't out to victimize an honest claimant, especially if that individual knows what they're doing!

Over the years the average insurance adjuster has been the recipient of many sad and stomach-churning experiences that have led them to become distrustful and downright cynical, regarding the individuals they deal with, day in and day out. This is a direct result of questionable and often weird accounts of circumstances and events routinely presented to them by both claimants and their own insured. In other words, the facts are so often distorted and misrepresented to them that they've developed a thick exterior to protect themselves from such nonsense. As a result some of them get "crusty." They become highly skeptical of what many of the individuals they are dealing with contend to be the gospel truth. Even when it *is,* they believe they're being told a gross prefabrication. This is very often the nature of that beast and you should be aware of it as you enter into an arena to do battle with him.

This pre-disposition causes many of them to resist claims. By and large, however, they are professionals. If you can document and justify the legitimacy of the value of your claim most of them will be inclined to pay you, close the case and move on. The adjuster's main concern is to be able to justify a settlement. He wants to satisfy himself, and his conscience, that he's paying what the claim is worth. And, *most importantly,* to be able to demonstrate to his superior that the payment he's made is plausible and documented by diagrams, statements, photographs, records, etc.

Adjusters are a group whom, as a professional class, have great respect for the individual who can demonstrate they're honest, informed, determined, well prepared and organized. It's in this theater of operation that your understanding of **The Baldyga**

**Auto Accident Settlement Evaluation Formula (BASE)** and the 4 "Values" it offers, will prove to be your most formidable weapon. That's because **BASE** will provide you with the greatest advantage possible for reaching a fair and equitable settlement of your personal injury claim. Armed with the knowledge you acquire from **BASE** you'll position yourself to aim for a sound demand and eventually negotiate a reasonable settlement.

## 3. THE ADJUSTER'S CLAIM LOAD

Adjusters are usually assigned a heavy load of new claims each month. Because of this they are continually working to close as many files as possible, *just to stay even.* When it comes to a case of clear liability they're under pressure to settle your claim - to get rid of it and move on. *Closing files and moving on!* These five words describe one of the basic elements of the insurance adjuster's work life. Keep in mind that the weight of their case load comes down on your side of the scale. Most people aren't aware of the advantage this holds for them.

Many adjusters often search for a way to finalize a case. Contrary to what many people assume, a typical adjuster is not determined to deny claims. His fixation is on terminating them. The easiest way to do this is to make a payment. When faced with a situation in which there's justification to support a payment his goal is to look for a way to get rid of it, rather than allow it to bubble and boil in Limbo.

The issue he's plagued with in settling a claim is to insure that whatever payment he's made can be substantiated. That is, to produce a file that will satisfy his superiors that the settlement justifies the payment made. This, in turn, provides the adjuster with the opportunity to close the case without the fear, after his superiors have reviewed his work, of a verbal sledge hammer crashing down upon him from high above. Contrary to public opinion most adjusters don't stay up nights attempting to create new ways to resist the payment of a claim. Their goal is not to deny a claim, regardless of all other considerations. The claims adjuster is a buyer of commodities. As such his goal is to wrangle as low a price as possible. A figure, to his way of thinking, that's fair. He wants to come up with one that will:

1. Be high enough to avoid frequent delays in the transaction.

2. Get the transaction concluded.

Rather than resisting the transactions, this buyer of commodities wants them to be supported by documents that will provide him with solid evidence of value received. If the intangible claim can be nailed down with medical bills, statements from employers, and similar documents of proof, the typical adjuster becomes a willing buyer. At that point what he needs, so as to be able to close the case and move on, is

69

for you to know what your claim is worth. **BASE** will tell you that and whichever of the 4 "Values" you've decide to aim for will be more than justified by the knowledge, documents, and reports you've learned about in this book. This is the kind of information you must be able to provide for him so he'll be in a position to prove to his superiors that what he paid you is acceptable.

Be pleasant but firm. No matter how much in the wrong the person is that hit you, no matter how they acted at the scene of the accident, and no matter what foolishness they may have verbalized to, or at you, don't take it out on the adjuster. It's not the adjuster's fault if the person who smashed into you is a chowderhead.

IT'S IMPORTANT TO REMEMBER: Never underestimate the value of the adjuster's impressions and conclusions about you. If he likes you, that's money in the bank. On the other hand, if they get upset at you, that information often ends up in your file. This data can sometimes be set in cement and, without your ever being aware of it, haunt you to the last day and the last dollar of your settlement.

As a general rule adjusters want to move cases. But, if they get upset at you, even if prudence and fairness dictates you should be paid right away, they can choose to sit on your claim *forever*. And, should they decide to pay you back for being unpleasant, bullheaded and/or impossible to speak, deal or reason with, that becomes a strong possibility.

## 4. THE INITIAL CONTACT

When you're first contacted avoid admitting or creating the impression you're fully recovered. And, if you're naturally a happy, gregarious sort, forget it! Get rid of your smile and laugh. Be reasonable and polite but you must keep reminding yourself that you're conducting serious business.

Don't be impossible to deal with but remain steady. Remember, the adjuster wants to look good to his company. He doesn't want your claim to end up in court, and he wants to reduce his claim load. Be patient. At the end of the day, after the dust settles, especially if you've correctly implemented **BASE**, he'll have no choice but to treat both you and your loss fairly.

## 5. YOUR STATEMENT - SIGNED OR RECORDED

If the insurance company calls you and suggests they take your statement over the telephone tell them you would prefer to meet with an adjuster, in person. Don't agree to dictate a verbal statement into a tape recorder over the telephone and certainly not when you're in the presence of an adjuster. Don't sign a statement when you meet

70

with him either. Whatever the circumstance may be, advise whomever you're dealing with that you'll be more than willing to provide a written or tape recorded statement, but only after your claim has been settled.

## 6. TAPE RECORD YOUR MEETINGS

When you meet and face each other you should tape record the discussion or, at the very least, take copious notes. It's wise to have a tape recorder present or a pen and notebook with you - but preferably, a tape recorder. Detailed notes or a tape will provide you with the opportunity to double-check everything that was said. Plus it will, right from the beginning, compel even the most negative type of adjuster (CHAPTER 9: HOW TO NEGOTIATE WITH AN ADJUSTER) to realize he's dealing with a claimant who is clear-headed, alert and on-the-ball. You can purchase a small, handheld "Dictaphone" mini-recorder at the electronics department of any Kmart, Wal-Mart, etc. for less than $50.

## 7. HAVE A WITNESS PRESENT

Each time you and the adjuster meet you should have a witness sit in. An adult friend or relative should be present. Choose someone - preferably not a spouse - who can attend each meeting, wherever it may take place. Introduce that individual as somebody you trust and want to sit in on your discussions. Having this witness present will keep both you and the adjuster from wandering too far from the subject matter at hand - which you should never do - because this often provides an adjuster with invaluable insights on how you can be manipulated.

## 8. EXAMINATION BY THE INSURANCE COMPANY DOCTOR

The adjuster may tell you he wants you to be examined by the doctor of his choice. Beware of such a request. Doctors assigned by the insurance company are notorious for finding nothing wrong with the claimant, and for stating, in the report they're paid to execute, that "there is no objective basis" for your complaints.

*You don't have to agree to be examined by the insurance company doctor!* The insurance company cannot insist that you submit to their doctor for an examination unless your claim actually becomes a formal court case.

Hold your ground until your attending physician has released you. After that it's okay to agree to be examined because by then it's *too late!* So much time will have passed it will be impossible for them to minimize the pain, discomfort and suffering your injury caused you.

# The BASE Formula
Baldyga Auto Accident Settlement Evaluation

Auto Accident Personal
Injury Insurance Claim

**CHAPTER 8**
© 2002 Daniel G. Baldyga

**The BASE Formula** is extremely easy to use. I developed this system over a period of years — in fact decades — as an insurance adjuster and claims manager and I can tell you that the settlement values that result from using **The BASE Formula** calculation will yield an aggressive yet achievable settlement value for your claim including "pain and suffering". The Formula will yield four initial values namely the low, middle, medium-high and high ranges of your claim value. I call these the Low Value, Core Value, Mean Value and Premium Value as follows. Please get familiar with this as it used throughout the Formula and this chapter.

| | |
|---|---|
| LOW VALUE | Low range |
| CORE VALUE | Medium range |
| MEAN VALUE | Medium-high range |
| PREMIUM VALUE | High range |

The four Values are listed above from lowest to highest simply for sake of simplicity. The four values provide a very solid minimum (Low Value) and fair maximum (Premium Value) to place your claim value "right in the ballpark". From there, you will use the information and examples I provide to objectively examine the unique conditions of your case (no two cases are exactly alike) and to determine which Value most closely represents what your claim is worth. In practice, you will begin your calculation with the CORE VALUE as a "starting point" and then you will add or subtract weight to the claim based on the circumstances and variables. Since there are typically more "variables" that could be added than subtracted, we start with the CORE Value which has one Value level below it and two Value levels above it.

These "variables" are discussed in further detail in this chapter but they include things such as the extent of your personal damage (visible bruises or scars, etc.), as well as the personal character, profession, age, and driving record of you and the other driver(s) involved in the accident. In other words if you are an unemployed ex-con, you are realistically going to deduct points and could end up at the Low Value whereas if you are a 70 year old retired school teacher who is loved in the community you're going to jump up to the Premium Value.    This is the reality of claims settlement at least in regard to the extent by which you can multiply or "factor up" your claim value.

I also provide you with sufficient insight and examples for you to understand why a claim will move from up or down through these four values.  And perhaps more importantly, I provide additional instruction throughout this book on how to take definitive action to move your claim "up a value" (such as through compiling effective photographs, negotiating tactics and so forth).

> The **BASE** calculation is predicated on the knowledge that in the vast majority of personal injury, motor vehicle accident cases, where the liability is undisputed and the soft-tissue injuries are basically similar, the settlement figure arrived at (give or take 10% to 20%) is usually two, three or four times Special Damages.

*"Special Damages" are all of those costs you have incurred (whether you've been paid by another source or not) not including your automobile repair cost.  These include hospital and doctor bills, ambulance charges, rental cars, etc. etc.  See Chapter Four for more discussion about what comprise Special Damages.*

> In other words,  typically the personal injury portion of a claim including "pain and suffering" can be but into a quick rough starting range by multiplying "Special Damages" (those costs not including property damage and as outlined in Chapter Four) by a MINIMUM of two and generally a maximum of four times.

However, there are various circumstances and variables that will come into play. You should read all of the examples in order to gain an understanding of what factors will apply to your situation.  Knowing that the range is from two to four (and maybe even five) times Special Damages and how to apply various variables to your advantage will place a very specific and realistic settlement value on your claim enabling you to negotiate hard with an adjuster to reach this number.

The following example illustrates **The BASE Formula** in action.

## INITIAL EXAMPLE AND FIRST STEP

 *SN*

We will assume that liability is clear and your Special Damages (excluding all property damages and motor vehicle repair costs) total $ 2,000. Remember, as indicated earlier in this book, your so-called Special Damages are your medical and non-medical monetary expenses.

We start by multiplying the $2,000 in Special Damages as follows:

| | | |
|---|---|---|
| 1. Low Value | Multiply Special Damages x 2.0 | 2.0 x $ 2,000 = $ 4,000 |
| 2. Core Value | Multiply Special Damages x 3.0 | 3.0 x $ 2,000 = $ 6,000 |
| 3. Mean Value | Multiply Special Damages x 3.5 | 3.5 x $ 2,000 = $ 7,000 |
| 4. Premium Value | Multiply Special Damages x 4.0 | 4.0 x $ 2,000 = $ 8,000 |

*normal UAM*

## As you can see above, the FIRST STEP is to multiply your Special Damages (see CHAPTER FOUR) by 2.0, 3.0, 3.5 and 4.0.

Then, assuming that the facts and particulars are "normal and routine" in your case, the claim (including "pain and suffering,") is worth The CORE Value. In the above example, the claim is assumed as "normal" with no special circumstances and is therefore worth the CORE Value of $ 6,000, *plus Property Damage*.

However, there are almost always at least some factors that can help push your claim toward the Mean Value. Each and every accident is unique. You must consider the facts and circumstances of your case to determine if you can move to the MEAN Value (slightly more than 50% of cases would typically move up to the MEAN Value) or even to the PREMIUM Value (about 15% of cases would justify this level). For example, if the other driver has a poor driving record or they were cited for drunken driving, or you have in your possession colored photographs that capture painful looking wounds on your body — under any of these conditions your case would have *extra* value and you would aim to settle it for as close as possible to The PREMIUM Value of $ 8,000.

On the other side of that coin, there could be a personal record of *your* past activities that includes outrageous conduct, of one sort or another, or other negative circumstances on your part (the liability is clear but you were found to have a loaded pistol or drugs in your motor vehicle) that have less than a favorable potential of your being awarded a fair settlement. If any such controversy raises its ugly head you may have no choice but to settle your case somewhere between The CORE Value of $ 6,000 and The LOW Value of $ 4,000.

Three examples follow to help you understand how the **BASE** Valuations work. Unless your case contains some bizarre or unspeakably adverse facts, that impact your case dramatically, you should never aim for a settlement below The LOW Value of $4,000 or in other words double the actual cost of your Special Damages. And conversely, in very special cases where there is an overwhelming collection of facts, photographs, evidence, etc. on your side, you could actually shoot for as high as FIVE times Special Damages (SUPER-PREMIUM if you will). **However, as stated above, a solid, typical and reasonable range for a normal claim is between 3 and 3.5 times Special Damages.**

## I.    THREE SETTLEMENT EVALUATION EXAMPLES

### EXAMPLE #1: SETTLEMENT VALUE - YOU'RE THE DRIVER

It's 10:00 AM on a clear, dry day. You're operating your Chevrolet Monte Carlo north on Main Street in your home town. You're 57 years old and the manager of a video store. Your son Chip is a passenger. Chip is a big, strong, young man who played varsity football in high school and college. He's currently home on Spring Break from graduate school where he's working on a Master's Degree.

Fred Fuddle is a chronically unemployed electrician with a reputation for being a loud-mouthed degenerate with a string of convictions for drunken, disorderly conduct. Fuddle is operating his dilapidated Ford pickup truck at a high rate of speed, driving East on Elm Street. As you approach the intersection of Main and Elm you have a green light.

Driving under the posted speed limit you proceed through the intersection. Too late, Fuddle realizes he has a red light. He hits his brakes, leaving over 50 feet of skid marks behind him as he zooms into the intersection. With a mighty crash the right front of his truck destroys the right rear of your car. Your left arm hits the steering wheel and the $300.00 wristwatch your spouse gave you for your last birthday is smashed. The Property Damage to your Monte Carlo will later be calculated to be $2,800.00.

The police investigate at the scene. Fuddle is charged with dangerous driving. That fact is stated in their accident report. Chip is transported to The Angel Of Mercy Hospital by a police cruiser. The officers at the scene don't think you look all that well. An ambulance is dispatched and you're brought to the same hospital. Once in the Emergency Room, you're x-rayed and examined. Diagnosis: A mild to severe sprain of the cervico-dorsal area - a typical "whiplash-type" injury.

Miraculously, considering the way Chip had been bounced around inside the Monte Carlo, he survived the accident with only a slight bump on his head and a sore elbow. However, his expensive prescription sunglasses are destroyed. It's determined there's no need for x-ray exams. Chip sees your family physician twice before returning to school.

Several hours after you're both home from the accident you ask Chip, who is well enough to get around, to return to the accident scene with his camera and snap photographs of the skid marks, plus the damage to your car. He does that. He also finds and takes photos of Fuddle's truck. Several weeks later you visit the police station where you obtain a copy of the report that the policewoman wrote at the scene. When you're finally released by your doctor, and you're ready to determine how much your case is worth, this is how your damages shape up.

At this point it would again be wise for the reader to go to the very end of APPENDIX D: After Impact Checklist and read "A Special Note." The information there will assist you in understanding the data and knowledge presented within the contents of this chapter and should help you to understand what's necessary to raise one "Value" *up* to the next Value level.

**DAMAGES**

**A.  SPECIAL DAMAGES**

| | |
|---|---|
| Lost Wages (2 weeks @ $648.00 per week) | $ 1,296.00 |
| Ambulance | 410.00 |
| Doctor's Final Bill | 485.00 |
| X-Rays | 215.00 |
| Prescription Medications For Pain | 58.00 ✓ |
| Heating Pad | 69.00 ✓ |

**TOTAL SPECIAL DAMAGES $ 2,533.00**

**B.  PROPERTY DAMAGE**

| | |
|---|---|
| Auto Repair | $ 2,800.00 |
| Wristwatch Replacement | 300.00 |

**TOTAL PROPERTY DAMAGE $ 3,100.00**

---

**CALCULATING THE SETTLEMENT VALUE FOR EXAMPLE I**

We apply **The BASE Formula** of evaluation by first multiplying the $2,533 in **Special Damages** as follow:

| | | | |
|---|---|---|---|
| **LOW VALUE** | 2.0 x | $ 2,533 = | $ 5,066 |
| **CORE VALUE** | 3.0 x | $ 2,533 = | $ 7,599 |
| **MEAN VALUE** | 3.5 x | $ 2,533 = | $ 8,865 |
| **PREMIUM VALUE** | 4.0 x | $ 2,533 = | $ 10,132 |

## Property Damage Is Separate

Remember, **The BASE Formula** addresses the Personal Injury portion of your claim. The property damage portion of our claim is $3,100. This does not change and is not included at all in the above valuation. Property Damages remain separate and are later added to the settlement of your personal injury claim.

## Narrowing the Range

The personal injury claim (as detailed above) is worth somewhere between a low of $5,066 and a high of $ 10,132. Now let's look at the particulars of this case to see how to narrow down this range.

Your case has a number of positive factors that come down on your side of the evaluation ledger. Fred Fuddle is far from being a model citizen. He was driving his vehicle much too fast, as evidenced by the skid marks Chip captured on film shortly after the accident. In addition to that the police cited Fuddle for operating his truck in a dangerous manner.

You know you have a solid reputation, and you can prove you were the victim of a tremendous impact, as evidenced by the photos Chip snapped of the Monte Carlo.

You have proof positive that you were unable to attend a national sales meeting of the video store chain you work for. A meeting that had in previous years led to greater profits being generated from your store and for you.

The doctor's report indicates you sustained a whiplash-type injury to the cervico-dorsal area. Following the doctors instructions you purchased a heating pad, which you used on and off for a week, to help relieve your pain and discomfort.

The adjuster knows there's an outside chance of your developing more neck problems related to the accident because of your age. He's also aware that you went through a great deal of inconvenience, together with the pain you suffered, and may still on occasion be forced to live with, as documented in your doctors report.

The cumulative effect of these facts is enough to place your claim in the area of The PREMIUM Value. You should aim for a settlement as close to The PREMIUM Value ($10,132) as possible, *plus* the $2,800.00 Property Damage to your Monte Carlo and the $300.00 replacement value of your wristwatch.

**This claim is worth about $13,232.**

**EXAMPLE #2: CHIP'S SETTLEMENT VALUE** A typical passenger's claim

## DAMAGES

**A.** **SPECIAL DAMAGES**
| | | |
|---|---|---|
| Doctor's Final Bill | $ | 265.00 |
| Emergency Room | | 208.00 |
| **TOTAL SPECIAL DAMAGES** | **$** | **473.00** |

**B.** **PROPERTY DAMAGE**
| | | |
|---|---|---|
| Prescription Sunglasses | | 162.00 |
| **TOTAL PROPERTY DAMAGE** | **$** | **162.00** |

---

## CALCULATING THE SETTLEMENT VALUE FOR EXAMPLE 2

We apply the BASE Formula of evaluation by first multiplying **Special Damages**:

| | | | |
|---|---|---|---|
| **LOW VALUE** | 2.0 x | $ 473 = | $ 946 |
| **CORE VALUE** | 3.0 x | $ 473 = | $ 1,419 |
| **MEAN VALUE** | 3.5 x | $ 473 = | $ 1,655 |
| **PREMIUM VALUE** | 4.0 x | $ 473 = | $ 1,892 |

Chip's claim also has a number of positive factors that come down on his side of the evaluation scale, although they are not as uniformly strong as yours because Chip only saw your family physician twice and his injuries, such as they were, are identified as "mild." He's an unusually healthy young man and would most likely have difficulty eliciting sympathy from a jury. Therefore, Chip's claim should be settled somewhere between The CORE Value of $1,419 and The MEAN Value of $1,655 — not including the $162.00 to replace his prescription sunglasses.

If Chip were a 75 year old man with a pre-existing arthritic condition that was aggrieved by this accident, even if he didn't have higher Special Damage's, the adjuster would have been delighted to pay The PREMIUM Value, perhaps even more, to get this settled and closed.

## EXAMPLE #3: SETTLEMENT VALUE - A DRIVER'S CLAIM

It's a cold winter day and snowing slightly. You're 22 years old, a married, full-time, at-home mom with two small children. Your mother is baby sitting for you and you've just concluded your weekly grocery shopping. You're now back inside your four year old Plymouth station wagon, in a mall parking lot with the door closed. You're fumbling in your pocketbook, attempting to retrieve your keys.

John Jones is a well-known, highly respected individual, who is now retired. He devotes many hours to his church where he holds the position of Deacon. He has two elderly women in his car with him. He's behind you, backing his year old Buick out of its parking space. Because of the snow that's accumulated on his rear window, he doesn't notice how close he's coming to your car. When he does he overly reacts. He stomps down on his brake pedal real hard but his wet boot slips off of it, down onto the gas pedal. The Jones Buick only travels a few feet but when his rear end smashes into your rear end there's a fairly powerful impact, enough to do $775.00 damage to your station wagon.

Not having buckled your seat belt as yet, you're bounced around inside your car, experiencing immediate pain in your shoulders and neck. Deacon Jones is beside himself with concern for your welfare. There's no need to call the police because the good Deacon admits to you, in the presence of his two passengers, that the accident is his fault. You get the ladies' names and addresses, just in case he changes his mind.

You don't feel it's necessary to go to the hospital emergency room, but when your husband arrives at the scene he insists you immediately proceed to the office of your family physician. Once there your doctor determines there's no need to take x-rays. You have bruise marks in your upper chest area. You're prescribed prescription pain killers and you go home. Your husband snaps photographs of your bruises. He makes sure to take photos of the damage to your station wagon and also Deacon Jones's Buick, which he later finds parked in the driveway of his home. Your husband relies on his own car for transportation to and from work. You need wheels in order to continue to accomplish your routine errands, but your station wagon is tied up for several days getting repaired. The motor repair shop has no "loaner" vehicles available. You have no choice but to rent a car for 5 days at $40.00 a day.

## DAMAGES

**A.   SPECIAL DAMAGES**

| | |
|---|---|
| Doctor's Bill | $    335.00 |
| X-Rays Taken By Doctor | 100.00 |
| Prescription Pain Medication | 85.00 |
| **TOTAL SPECIAL DAMAGES** | **$    520.00** |

**B.   PROPERTY DAMAGE**

| | |
|---|---|
| Auto Repair | $    775.00 |
| Rental Car | 200.00 |
| **TOTAL PROPERTY DAMAGE** | **$    975.00** |

---

### CALCULATING THE SETTLEMENT VALUE FOR EXAMPLE 3

We apply the BASE Formula of evaluation by first multiplying **Special Damages**:

| | | | |
|---|---|---|---|
| **LOW VALUE** | 2.0 x | $ 520 = | **$  1,040** |
| **CORE VALUE** | 3.0 x | $ 520 = | **$  1,560** |
| **MEAN VALUE** | 3.5 x | $ 520 = | **$  1,820** |
| **PREMIUM VALUE** | 4.0 x | $ 520 = | **$  2,080** |

Special Damages total $520.00.   As always, the property damage is excluded from calculating the personal injury portion of the claim and is added at the end.    Now let's look at the details of the situation to see how we can narrow this range:

Both you and Deacon Jones have excellent reputations. Nonetheless, you received a substantial blow when he backed into you. Your physical distress never got to the point where you had to lay down and rest. However, you did experience several days of mild pain, followed by several more of subtle discomfort.    Your case should be settled at The MEAN Value of $1,820.00, perhaps a bit higher, but certainly no less. In addition, Jones' insurance company must also pay you $775.00 for the damage to your Plymouth, plus $200.00 for the five day rental of another car while yours was being repaired.

## BASE SUMMARY

That's how **The BASE Formula** is calculated, constructed and implemented. If, after digesting all of the above, **BASE** looks to be fairly easy to execute, you're right!   IT IS!!!

The key here is the fact that I have been dealing with  Auto Accident Claims for over half of my lifetime and I have found (over the years and decades plus multi-thousands of cases settled both in and out of court) that this range of value is absolutely consistent.

**BASE** places the claim in a position to be settled not immediately but after some negotiation to the high range of what the claim is worth and what will eventually be paid by the insurance company – time and time again.

*Dan Baldyga*

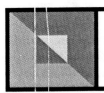
## I.    THE "REASONABLE" FACTOR

You should meet an adjuster's reasonable questions with prudent answers. But, be careful, because some questions aren't legitimate - sometimes they may be intended to learn something that has the potential to influence you to settle your claim for less than it's worth.   There's a simple negotiation rule to follow: If the inquiry seems reasonably necessary for the adjuster to obtain an accurate picture and assessment of your claim, be sensible in your response. But, if you're not sure whether a question is logical or not, say "I'm not certain that's a reasonable request." Wait and allow him to explain why it is !

When it comes to this particular issue you're going to have to consider both sides of the negotiating process. Bear in mind, a claims adjuster has no legal right to see or receive anything specific, or insist that you answer anything in particular.   On the other hand, the claims adjuster is not legally obligated to settle a claim. In order to bring it to a conclusion he must have sufficient information so as to understand the facts of the accident, your injuries, and your damages. You should balance your reluctance to provide him with too much information against his need to properly evaluate your claim.

## 2.  THE NEGOTIATION PROCESS IN ACTION

Negotiating a final settlement is like attending a flea market and bargaining for something that attracts your attention at one of the booths. You and the buyer (the adjuster) both have a fairly good idea how much an item (your injury) is worth. Because of **BASE**, and the 4 "Values" you've calculated, you know how much you're willing to take for it and the adjuster has a pretty good idea how much his company is willing to pay. But, just like at the flea market, neither of you really knows to what limits the other side is willing to go. And so, like it or not, you have no choice but to engage in the give-and-take process of testing each other. It usually proceeds something like this:

Let's assume that as a result of your application of **The BASE Formula** you've decided to aim for The MEAN Value, and that figure is $8,700.00, plus your Property Damage. That's the bottom-line amount you've concluded you should aim for in order to obtain a fair and legitimate settlement.

When negotiating always show the adjuster you're willing to do so in good faith and that you understand the process. Your initial demand for settlement should be approximately two times the value you choose. So, in this particular case, your initial demand would be (2 X $8,700) = $17,400, plus your Property Damage.

More often than not your initial demand is going to shock the adjuster into reality. Once there he's going to take a deep breath and say to himself, "This guy knows what he's doing."

The first rule of bargaining with the adjuster is, *never lower your demand until the adjuster makes a counter-offer*. If you lower your demand once or twice during a single negotiation contact (either in person or in a telephone conversation) without the adjuster making a counter-offer, you've revealed to him that your initial demand is weak. A good rule-of-thumb to always keep in mind is: If you lower your demand you should wait until the adjuster makes a counter-offer before reducing your demand a second time.

Think of your negotiation process as similar to selling a car or any other property. You initially ask for more than you're willing to accept and the potential buyer offers less than they're willing to pay. After some negotiations, you settle on a price somewhere in the middle making both parties feel as if they got a reasonably good deal.

Negotiating a settlement for your insurance claim is much like any other negotiation. You're the "seller" and the adjuster is the "buyer." In essence what you're doing is selling the value of your claim to the insurance company through their representative - the claims adjuster.

BE PATIENT! A claim settled in haste is rarely paid its fair and full value.

After you've made your initial demand the adjuster may begin to bargain then and there, or he may ask for some time to consider your demand, and then get back to you, either in person or by telephone. One way or the other he'll say something like, "You've asked for $17,400 plus your Property Damage. Come on now, you know that's not realistic. What can we really settle this case for, right now?"

Your response should be something like, "Ok, so you tell me what it's worth. I'd really like to settle it." This answer is truthful. What you've said doesn't scare the adjuster away and you've not given up anything. You've left the door open for the counter-offer you really want.

If the adjuster offers you anything over what the figure that **The BASE Formula** has indicated your claim is worth, settle it then and there. (The chance of this coming to pass is about one in a gazillion)!

If he says something like, "I can offer you $5,000 plus your Property Damage," this implies he's got more. Most of the time an adjuster's counter-offer, especially his first one, is negotiable. But, there's only one way to find out. Your response should be, "Is that figure your maximum authority?" Now, you're asking him to bid against himself. You're not committing yourself to a lower figure than your initial demand. What you're doing is obtaining valuable information.

Typically the adjuster will say something like, "No, that's not my maximum authority. But you'll have to get into my ballpark if we're going to settle this claim." He's telling you he has more money but he wants you to come down before he offers it. You should, at this point, come down about twenty percent (in this particular example that would be about $13,920) and then try something like this on for size, "I still believe my case is worth a lot more than what you're offering me but I'm willing to come down a little."

At that point you might pause thoughtfully and then add, "I've been waiting a long time now and I'd really like to get this over with. I'll settle for $13,920."

This back-and-forth process continues until you and the adjuster barter a settlement to somewhere in the vicinity of $8,700. Maybe more? It's usually as simple, and drawn out, as that. The main facts that determine how accident settlement's are resolved are:

1.  How much you know your claim is worth, thanks to what **BASE** has revealed to you:

    The LOW Value

    The CORE Value

    The MEAN Value

    The PREMIUM Value

    You've determined which of these "Values" you're going to settle at and why.

2.  How well you've prepared each stage of your claim: Investigation, the gathering of supporting documents and reports, photographs, etc.

3.  How much of a hurry you're in to settle.

## 3. BE WILLING TO WAIT

Try not to be in a hurry to settle your claim. Don't jump at the first offer. Holding back often increases your settlement amount. In almost every instance the passage of time is on your side. If you're patient you'll discover the adjuster will want to move your claim, sooner rather than later. Because of this you have a much better chance to obtain the "Value" for which you are aiming.

## 4. STAY ON TOP OF YOUR CLAIM

Don't let the adjuster, for whatever reasons, sit on your case, If he said he'll be doing something like checking back with his supervisor, etc., you should agree upon a specific date by which that will be done. It's a good idea to put whatever it is you've agreed upon in a confirming letter and send it to him. When that specific date rolls around contact him and politely request a response. If you have, for example, lowered your settlement demand, agree upon a reasonable deadline by which you would expect a response. In other words, make sure the adjuster knows you're out there in the real world waiting for him to make the next move. Make it clear to him you're going to stay on top of your claim until it's settled.

## 5. BE STRAIGHT

Insurance adjusters don't respond well to abuse or hysterics. On the other hand they'll listen if they believe you understand what you're talking about. Let the adjuster know you believe in the facts you've presented, and in the "Value" **BASE** has provided you for your "pain and suffering." Stick to your guns but avoid extreme and negative emotions. In most instances, if you demonstrate to the adjuster that you're making a good faith claim, the odds are you'll eventually achieve a fair and honest settlement.

## 6. HANDLING THE "NEGATIVE" ADJUSTER

A few adjusters are unreasonable and impossible to deal with. Unfortunately that's their nature. They're not going to change. No matter what you prove to them, or how reasonable you are, they will remain negative right from the beginning to the bitter end.

If bad luck has stuck you with somebody like that you must remain cool, calm and unflappable. Just as you would have done even if he wasn't so negative, you should proceed to present to that adjuster the provable and legitimate figures you've accumulated: Your bills, your costs and your expenses, all of which are a direct result of the accident.

Be firm about being allowed your *gross* wage loss and not your *net* wage loss. Permit no discussions regarding sick leave benefits, even if you've been paid your wages by your employer or been reimbursed your wages from some other insurance coverage(s) you may have. In many states, if you're self-employed, even if you didn't lose a penny out-of-pocket, your "lost earning capacity" is a legitimate consideration and becomes a strong factor in helping to justify your evaluation figure.

This possible confrontation can turn out to be a blessing in disguise because that negative adjuster is going to get the message that you aren't a pushover. He's going to come to realize that you know how to evaluate your claim and you're not going away until you've obtained a fair and reasonable settlement.

You're entitled to full and honest payment of your losses. Insisting on getting every dollar owed to you is your absolute right. The negative adjuster may try the wily device of accusing you of being "greedy" or "trying to make a profit" from the accident. If they attempt this sort of hocus-pocus you should respond with something like, "I think fairness dictates I should be paid every penny that's legally owed to me. No amount of money will ever compensate me for the pain and suffering I've been subjected to because of this accident."

## 7. SETTLEMENT AUTHORITY

Whether he falls into that small minority of negative adjuster or the large majority of professional adjuster, when he comes to realize you understand how much your claim is worth, you and he will eventually come to an agreement as to the settlement amount. Once you and the adjuster agree on a figure, he'll ask you to sign a "release" to finalize the settlement.

The adjuster's authority to settle claims on their own is usually restricted to certain dollar limits. These limits depend on how much experience that adjuster has. Those who haven't been around too long may have an authority of $5,000 to $10,000. The more experienced adjuster, perhaps as high as $25,000.

An adjuster will rarely come right out and tell you what his authority is unless he finds himself in a position where he may have to make an offer higher than his limit. If so, he'll have to ask for approval from his supervisor or manager. If he tells you he must check with a superior, regarding the settlement figure, be sure to decide upon a date by which you'll hear back from him. Once you've done that, send him a letter confirming the date you and he agreed upon.

87

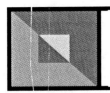

# Stalemate!
## You and the Adjuster Agree To Disagree

You tried to settle your motor vehicle accident insurance claim but you've hit a brick wall while attempting to negotiate the value of your claim. What are your options? What can you do? What must you know? To discover the answer to these questions you ought to be acquainted with the following:

## 1. GOING OVER THE ADJUSTER'S HEAD

If you've reached an impasse, because the adjuster fails to pay you the value you've placed on your claim, politely suggest that your differences might be overcome if you both got another opinion, and ask to speak with his supervisor. Asking the adjuster to bring his immediate superior into the picture may influence him to change his offer.  If the adjuster promises to contact his supervisor for a review of the file, you should allow two or three weeks to pass. After he and his supervisor have had a chance to discuss your case the adjuster will often come back with a better offer.

If nothing comes of the above, call the insurance company. You know the adjuster's name. Advise the operator you would like to talk to that adjuster's supervisor. Be sure to have your claim number, the name of their insured, and any other relevant information he may ask for to help him locate your file.

You'll usually find the supervisor will be inclined to chat.  One of his major responsibilities is to do everything he can to reduce his department's claim load.  Under normal circumstances he'll be happy to get rid of your case because you're just one of *thousands*!  Be prepared to allow him some time to examine your file. He'll probably not be familiar with your claim and will ask to call you back so he can review the facts before proceeding. That's a legitimate and reasonable request.

Do you feel the adjuster hasn't been treating you right? If so keep that to yourself. Don't be nasty or arrogant. It's OK to be firm but you should also be kind and gracious. Don't knock your adjuster. Simply ask his supervisor if there's a way you and he can reach a value on your case and get it settled. More often that not this approach works, especially if your adjuster has a reputation for being excessively negative, hard-nosed, lazy, difficult to deal with, or a combination of those traits which a few insurance adjusters acquire over the years.  If you can't obtain a reasonable settlement offer from the supervisor, ask him or her to give you in writing the reasons for the insurance company's position. This statement may be helpful in any further steps you have to take.

## 2. SMALL CLAIMS COURT

Every state has a Small Claims Court that provides a simple, quick, inexpensive and informal procedure for resolving cases involving relatively small amounts of money. Some Small Claims Courts are called Conciliation Court, Justice Court, the Small Claims Division, or Docket of the Municipal or District Court.

If Small Claims Court turns out to be a practical alternative, the documents you've already collected, and the work you've already done in presenting your demand to the adjuster, will be nearly all the preparation you'll need to have your case heard. Once you get to Small Claims Court you'll present the same facts and make the same argument as you made to the adjuster, only now a neutral judge will be listening.

Small Claims Court is often referred to as the "User Friendly" court. Most cases are filed and decided without lawyers. The amount of the award the court can make is limited by state statutes (for example: Ohio $3,000, Rhode Island $1,500 or Connecticut $2,500). You should check this out. If you're looking for $5,000 and their limit is $3,000 there's no sense to proceed.

In states with a high dollar limit in small Claims Court (for example: Delaware, $15,000; Minnesota, $7,500; Pennsylvania, $8,000; Virginia, $15,000) simply filing a Small Claims Court action, and serving the papers on the person who caused the accident, might stimulate the insurance company to raise its offer.

If the Small Claims Court dollar limit is much higher than what the insurance company has offered, the company has to face the possibility that its insured will lose and be told to pay you up to the dollar limit of that particular court. This may prompt a new and higher settlement offer. Extra pressure to settle the claim might also come from their insured, who will be upset about having to go to court, especially on a case when there's no question of who was at fault. Rather, the question is how much money should be paid to you for the "pain and suffering" they caused you.

See APPENDIX H: State Listing Of Small Claims Court Limits. Here you will find the current dollar limits for each state's Small Claims Court. Be careful because the limit in your state may have changed, or there may be local variances which permit a higher or lower limit in certain counties. Before filing, call the Small Claims clerk to double-check what their specific and latest monetary limit is.

## 2.1. Organizing Documents

Because a judge can accept written evidence and would prefer things on paper, which he can refer to, bring these documents with you to court. Bring three copies of each for possible distribution to other parties.

1. The police report

2. All helpful witness statements

3. Photographs

4. Your medical bills

5. Your medical reports

6. Proof of your lost wages and lost earning capacity

7. Letters, or any other documents, which show or help to explain all other losses you suffered as a result of your injuries

## 2.2. Preparing An Oral Statement

Small Claims Court judges usually only want to hear a brief statement of your claim. Plan on presenting your claim in no more than five minutes. State as simply as possible:

1. What kind of an accident you had

2. Where and when the accident happened

3. What your injuries were, emphasizing the "pain and suffering" you experienced because of those injuries

4. The treatment you received (hand him a copy of your Medical Report)

5. The length of your Total Disability and/or your Partial Disability

6. How much your medical treatment cost, regardless of whether you paid for it yourself, or some other insurance coverage paid for it

7. How much income you lost

8.    Any other damages or inconveniences you may have suffered as a result of the accident

9.    How much compensation you believe is fair and reasonable

Make sure the settlement figure you're asking for is higher than what you believe the case is worth. If the amount you're seeking is higher than the dollar limit for that particular Small Claims Court, explain to the judge what you believe your case is worth and then state you're aware of the small claims limit of that court, so you're asking for the maximum allowed.

### 2.3. Go Visit A Claims Court In Session

It would be wise to visit a Small Claims Court in session so you can observe how other people present their cases and to note the kinds of questions the judge asks.

### 2.4. Disadvantages Of Small Claims Court

Once you go to Small Claims Court, your claim has been concluded. Whatever happens in Small Claims Court will be the final outcome of your entire claim. By going to Small Claims Court, attempting to obtain up to that particular court's dollar limit, you've usually given up the right to collect any value beyond that limit.

### 2.5. Lawsuit Deadlines

As discussed in CHAPTER ONE each state puts a time limit, called a Statue of Limitations, on how long you have to bring suit. (See APPENDIX B: Statutes of Limitation). *Be careful and WATCH OUT* because these limitations (in some states you have only a year) will usually apply to that state's particular Small Claims Court also.

## 3.  CONTACTING THE STATE DEPARTMENT OF INSURANCE

The mere mention of filing a complaint with the state department of insurance may bring the adjuster around to making a fair settlement offer. But if it doesn't, you should file an actual complaint. Send them a letter which includes:

1.    The date of the accident and the people involved

2.    A general description of your claim

3. The insurance company's claim number

4. Details of the difficulties you've had with the adjuster. For example, long delays, an unfair settlement offer, improper tactics, etc.

5. The number of conversations you've had with the adjuster, or his supervisors, in your attempt to settle the matter

6. Copies of all documents and reports so the insurance department investigator will understand how you arrived at your value

When this process begins someone in the claims department of the insurance company, other than the adjuster who handled your claim, will become aware that you're a claimant who intends to do whatever it takes to do whatever it takes not to be taken advantage of and to obtain a fair and reasonable settlement. That often inspires them to take another look at your claim and come up with a better offer. Also, because a complaint with the state department of insurance adds another layer of extra work the insurance company has to perform, they may try harder to settle your claim.

## 4. THE THREAT OF A LAWSUIT

Neither insurance companies, nor their adjusters, are going to sing, whistle, shout, or leap up and click their heels in glee when presented with a lawsuit. That's emphatically true when there's no doubt the legal action had nothing to do with liability but was brought *only because* of a dispute regarding value! Lawyers are going to get involved, costs will skyrocket and the claim file may be taken away from the adjuster, and given to somebody else to handle, which could mean a blemish on that adjuster's work record.

Since a claims adjuster wants to avoid all this, you might be able to loosen his purse strings by suggesting that if a fair offer isn't made by a certain date, you'll have no choice but to hire an attorney and file a lawsuit.

No adjuster in his right mind wants that to happen, *especially* in a case where there's no question that their insured is 100% responsible for the accident.

93

No-Fault automobile insurance law is most often referred to in policies as Personal Injury Protection (PIP). Whether you have No-Fault coverage and the amount of PIP benefits you carry - that is the amount of medical bills and lost income your own company will pay regardless of who is at fault in the accident - depends on your individual insurance policy. To make certain whether you have PIP coverage, and to determine what your PIP benefits are, read your policy carefully. If your policy includes PIP protection, file your first claim for injury compensation - medical costs and lost income only, up to the dollar limit of your coverage - with your own insurance company, following the procedures detailed in the PIP section of your policy.

Explaining No-Fault insurance, in simple terms, and covering the whole United States, is beyond the scope of this book. However, the contents of this chapter is an attempt to provide the reader with generalized insights. Should you find yourself an auto-crash victim in a No-Fault state, you should seek information and help from your insurance agent regarding your coverage and the impact on the various and particular aspects of your claim. In some states, the No-Fault system requires that in exchange for your being able to count on what is an almost automatic payment for damages from *your own* insurance company, there's a possibility you've given up the right to recover an additional amount of money for your "pain and suffering." In some states, however, you may recover for "pain and suffering," if your claim meets a certain threshold. A given state, for example, may required you to have sustained injuries with over $500 in medical bills before you can seek compensation for your "pain and suffering."

## I. STATES WITH NO-FAULT JURISDICTIONS
* Data Compiled 1999 so you should double check this list

The following 24 states have some form of No-Fault Motor Vehicle Insurance Law:

| | | | |
| --- | --- | --- | --- |
| Arkansas | Georgia | Michigan | Pennsylvania |
| Colorado | Hawaii | Minnesota | S Carolina |
| Connecticut | Kansas | New Jersey | South Dakota |
| Delaware | Kentucky | New York | Texas |
| District of Columbia | Maryland | North Dakota | Utah |
| Florida | Massachusetts | Oregon | Virginia |

No-Fault is a concept by which your own insurance company is required to pay for your losses for bodily-injury, without regard to who is at fault in the accident. It consolidates damages for all your medical expenses growing out of an auto accident, plus your lost earnings, requiring them to be reimbursed to you by your own insurance company, without regard to fault.

This type of coverage is also involved in property damages, in the sense that insured motorists in any given No-Fault state can purchase collision coverage to pay for damages to their cars and only enough Property Damage liability to protect them when driving outside their state. The plan requires, however, that in exchange for being able to count on an automatic payment for damages from your own insurance company - without arguing about who's at fault - you give up your right to recover a monetary reward for the "pain and suffering" you were subjected to because of the injuries you received in the accident.

You don't have to give up this right in all situations. You'll probably have to do so when it comes to smaller cases but you often retain that right in cases involving more than minor injuries. For example, the law in one particular state may require that you sustain injuries in excess of $1,000 in medical bills, before you can negotiate compensation for your "pain and suffering."

The circumstances under which you can file a liability claim vary from No-Fault state to No-Fault state. To make up for what PIP benefits do not cover, most No-Fault laws also permit an injured driver to file a liability claim, and lawsuit if necessary, against the driver who was at fault in an accident. The liability claim allows an injured driver to obtain compensation for medical and income losses above and beyond what the PIP benefits have paid, as well as for "pain and suffering" and other general damages. Whether you can file a liability claim depends on the specifics of the No-Fault law in your state.

Under some PIP policies, if you file a liability claim and recover damages after you also collected PIP benefits, your own PIP insurance company has a right to be reimbursed by you for the amount it paid you. Under other No-Fault policies, your PIP insurance company does not have a right to reimbursement from you but it does have a right of "subrogation." Subrogation meaning it can recover your PIP benefits directly from the insurance company of the individual that smashed into you.

## WHAT HAPPENS WHEN THE INSURANCE OF THE PERSON AT FAULT DOESN'T FULLY COVER THE OTHER PERSON'S DAMAGES?

It depends on whether the negligent person has enough assets to cover your damages. If you think they do (the chances that this person will pay you without a fight are very remote) you will probably have no other choice than to hire an attorney and *sue* that person directly in your attempt to recover.

You can protect yourself in advance by purchasing "*under*insurance coverage", which pays for uncovered damage caused by other drivers who have only the bare minimum of insurance. This will fill the gap between what the other individual's insurance will pay and what you're shelling out for repairs, medical bills and all other out-of-pocket expenses.

## WHAT HAPPENS WHEN AN INSURED DRIVER HAS AN ACCIDENT WITH AN *UNINSURED* PERSON, AND THE ACCIDENT IS THE OTHER'S FAULT?

In a No-Fault state, your insurer automatically covers you. In other states, there are sanctions for not having insurance. In some states, it is illegal not to have insurance. If you have a collision with an uninsured driver and the police are called, the state may fine or even arrest that person. You can protect yourself against such expensive run-ins by making sure that your own policy contains "*un*insured motorist coverage" which allows you to make a claim for damages by the *un*insured. Some states also maintain an *un*insured motorist fund, which you can apply to if you have damages that are not covered. There will, however, be a limit to how much you can collect. For further information read "Uninsured And Underinsured Motorist Coverage" found in CHAPTER 12.

## 2. "ADD ON", "MONETARY THRESHOLD", "SERIOUS INJURY THRESHOLD"

Some states have what are the so-called "Add-On" No-Fault laws that put no restrictions on your right to file a liability claim in addition to your PIP claim. In these states, you can file a liability claim against the person at fault for all damages in excess of your PIP benefits. Other No-Fault states have different types of "thresholds" that an injured person must arrive at, pass through and exceed before they can file a claim for full compensation. Some states have a "Monetary Threshold" only and some a "Serious Injury Threshold" only. Some have both. Often those with both thresholds allow a liability claim to be made if an injured person meets either one.

### 2.1. States With "Add On" Coverage
* Data Compiled 1999 so you should double check this list

| | | |
|---|---|---|
| Arkansas | Oregon | South Dakota |
| Delaware | Pennsylvania | Texas |
| Maryland | South Dakota | Virginia |

In the 9 states listed above you have a right to file a liability claim against the other driver or owner *in addition* to your PIP insurance. This kind of PIP coverage is "added on" to an injured persons rights under traditional liability law.

In these states, a liability claim is handled exactly the same as a claim in a typical Fault state. Because of this you can follow all the information and directions contained within this book regarding **The BASE Formula** and negotiating a settlement of your liability claim.

## 3. "CHOICE" NO-FAULT
* Data Compiled 1999 so you should double check this list

> Kentucky
> New Jersey
> Pennsylvania

In these three states, the motorist has a choice: He may elect to reject the threshold and maintain an unrestricted right to recover for economic damages and also "pain and suffering." Or choose to retain the ability to get recovery for economic damages, while *limiting the ability* to recover any additional dollars for their "pain and suffering."

## 4. STATES WITH "MONETARY THRESHOLDS"
* Data Compiled 1999 so you should double check this list

| | |
|---|---|
| Colorado | $2,500 |
| District of Columbia | PIP benefit amount |
| Hawaii | PIP benefit amount |
| Kansas | $ 500 |
| Kentucky | $1,000 |
| Massachusetts | $ 500 |
| Minnesota | $4,000 |
| North Dakota | $2,500 |
| Utah | $1,000 |

The No-Fault laws in the nine states listed above permit a liability claim against the individual at fault whenever the injured person has medical expenses over a certain limit. The Medical Expense Threshold limit is listed next to each state. Please note: these are 1999 figures so you should double check to make sure these Monetary Thresholds are correct.

Once you've reached that threshold, you're free to file a routine liability claim against those who are at fault for your accident. All of these states also permit a liability claim if a certain "Injury Threshold" (discussed below) is met instead of the above stated "Monetary Threshold" which is often referred to as the Medical Expense Threshold.

Medical expenses that count toward reaching the "Monetary Threshold" include not only ambulance, hospital, emergency room, clinic, doctor, nursing, and laboratory but also dental work, physical therapy and chiropractic. To discover what is counted toward the threshold limit in your state, read the definition of medical expense in your No-Fault (PIP) insurance policy.

## 5. STATES WITH "SERIOUS INJURY" THRESHOLDS
* Data Compiled 1999 so you should double check this list

The thirteen states listed below permit an injured person to file a liability claim against those at fault in an accident if you had a serious injury, regardless of how much money was spent on medical treatment. Injuries that qualify as serious are defined by each state's law. If you meet your state's injury threshold, you may proceed to follow all the other information and direction presented in this book regarding **The BASE Formula**, as well as how one should go about filing, negotiating and settling their claim.

| | |
|---|---|
| Colorado | Massachusetts |
| District Of Columbia | Michigan |
| Florida | Minnesota |
| Hawaii | New Jersey |
| Kansas | New York |
| Kentucky | North Dakota |
| | Utah |

## 6. THE BOTTOM LINE REGARDING NO-FAULT

At first blush it may appear that those who have injury-producing accidents in No-Fault states may be excluded from taking advantage of the information found in this book and **The BASE Formula**. But, between the "Add On" No-Fault states, the "Choice" No-Fault states, plus the states without No-Fault laws, there are a total of 39 states whose citizens can apply the information contained in this book.

Even those states which seem to be left in the ranks of pure No-Fault cannot truly be considered No-Fault states by the strictest interpretation. They too have a number of various, sometimes complicated, thresholds which, once met, allow you to take advantage of the knowledge you've gained from this book, *plus* **BASE**, to assist you in obtaining all that you are entitled to.

---

### IN CONCLUSION

If you're in a No-Fault state, before you can proceed to evaluate and settle your case, you must carefully read all that's stated under the Personal Injury Protection (PIP) section of your insurance policy. If you have any questions you should check with your insurance agent about how to determine what your restrictions are and how to chart your course. In many instances, even though your accident occurred in a No-Fault state, you can proceed as outlined in this book.

On the other hand, if your accident occurred within the boundaries of a Fault state, you're unencumbered from the moment of impact. Armed with the information in this book, and with the implementation of **The BASE Formula**, you can proceed to document, evaluate and negotiate a settlement of your claim for personal injuries.

---

## ONE LAST TIME, THE READER IS CAUTIONED TO NOTE

In this chapter, wherever you observe an asterisk (*) displayed, together with the notation "Data Compiled " (with a date inserted) it's important for you to note that such statistics are subject to change. For that reason the information must be double-checked. You can do so by contacting the Department Of Insurance to determine if indeed the Fault and No-Fault information that's important to you is still correct.

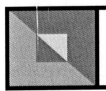

There are a number of insurance coverages, other than those listed below, that have little, if any, relevance when it comes to an insurance claim when the liability is clear. Since we're concentrating on accidents where fault is not an issue, to concentrate on these would be non-productive.

As stated throughout this book the contents of these pages is about *evaluating* the "pain and suffering" one is subjected to because of Soft Tissue injuries. In other words, placing a value on a trauma that's the direct result of an impact where there's *no question* who is at fault.

However, it would be prudent to touch briefly on the following:

## I. PROPERTY DAMAGE LIABILITY COVERAGE

Property Damage Liability Coverage pays for the damage one causes to another's property. This coverage is usually sold in a combination with Bodily Injury Liability Coverage and is limited to a certain amount, as stated on the policy. Typically, you're expected to submit to the insurance company two, or more, estimates of damage, from reputable auto body shops.

## 2. COMPREHENSIVE COVERAGE

Comprehensive personal liability coverage is a catch-all that pays for damages resulting from just about everything, except collision with another car, or crashing into a solid object like a tree, telephone pole, or retaining wall. It provides personal liability coverage for members of your family. It also offers other persons protection for their liability arising out of their use of your vehicle, and further provides medical payments, without regard to who's negligent or at fault, for persons who are injured in an accident involving your vehicle or you.

Comprehensive coverage also pays to repair the damage to your car for causes other than collision. For example: Flood, Fire (Explosion), Hail, Theft, Vandalism, Windstorm (Hurricane). It does not apply to wear and tear, mechanical breakdown or freezing. This particular coverage is usually subject to deductibles.

## 3. COLLISION COVERAGE

Collision coverage pays to repair the damage to your car when caused by a collision with another motor vehicle or object, even if the accident is your fault. Collision payments are also subject to a deductible. An overwhelming number of vehicles are covered by collision insurance. If you do have this particular coverage it means:

1.   You have the right to collect payment for your damaged motor vehicle, no matter who was at fault, by filing a claim against your own insurance company; but you must pay the deductible.

2.   The sum that matters (i.e. the amount it will cost you) is the deductible. Your insurance company will have you sign a Subrogation Agreement. This will allow them to be reimbursed ("subrogated") if and when you settle with the other driver's insurance company. On the other hand, if you're at fault, you'll not get back whatever you paid for your deductible.

## 4. UNINSURED AND UNDERINSURED MOTORIST COVERAGE

Uninsured and/or Underinsured Motorist Coverage pays for both you and your passenger's medical expenses, loss of income, *plus* the "pain and suffering" caused by an uninsured or underinsured driver. These two coverages are designed to protect you, your car, your passengers and your assets, but not others whom you injured.

### UNINSURED MOTORIST COVERAGE (UMC)

This coverage is now required by statue in almost every state. It will reimburse you for any bodily injury, and medical expenses, or even death (but not property damage) that you or anyone in your vehicle may sustain from a motor vehicle accident. For example, accidents caused by a hit-and-run driver, or the driver of a stolen car, or a driver who has no insurance. UMC provides you protection against any bodily injury you sustain from an accident with a motorist who has no motor vehicle insurance coverage.

Most UMC will pay up to the stated limits for bodily injuries caused to:

1.   You, or a relative who lives with you, while a driver or passenger in the vehicle named in your policy, or in any other vehicle you don't own, or while a pedestrian.

2.   Anyone else driving your insured vehicle with your permission and anyone riding in your vehicle who is named in your insurance policy. Plus any other vehicle you're driving, but don't own.

102

UMC normally has rules limiting your ability to collect compensation, and the amount you receive, as follows:

1.    If your accident is with a hit-and-run driver, you must notify the police within twenty-four hours of the accident. Also, if your accident *is* the result of a hit-and-run driver, most policies require that your vehicle was actually struck by the other car. That means your being forced off the road, but not struck, by a driver who disappears, and is never seen or heard of again, is not sufficient.

2.    If you're injured on the job, your UMC payments will be reduced by the workers' compensation, or any other disability payments.

3.    If you receive payments for medical bills from your own insurance company under Medical Payments Coverage, the amount you're entitled to recover under UMC is secondary.

If you file a claim under your UMC, an adjuster from your own insurance company will handle your claim exactly as if it were a routine liability claim. At that point, **The BASE Formula** kicks in because you'll be negotiating with that adjuster for the *additional payment*, of your "pain and suffering."


## UNDERINSURED MOTORIST COVERAGE

(If you're allowed to purchase this coverage you should). Some drivers carry enough insurance to meet their state's minimum liability insurance coverage requirements but not enough to cover all their damages. If the other driver has some insurance, the Underinsured Coverage, as stated in your policy, may allow you to be compensated - *beyond* what the other driver's limits will pay. And, just like UMC, **The BASE Formula** should be set up, calculated and executed, to determine the 4 "Value's" of your "pain and suffering."

Once you've settled a claim with the other driver's insurance company for the maximum on that policy, confer with your Underinsured Coverage company about how much more than this amount your case may be worth. Up to the extent of your Underinsurance policy limits, you can negotiate to collect this extra amount from your own company. It's important to note that any dollars you received from your insurance company, via your Medical Payments Coverage, will be deducted from the amount you collect from your Underinsured Coverage.

To collect from your Underinsured Motorist Coverage, you must first show your insurance company that the person who struck you was underinsured for the damage they caused. You should obtain from the other driver's insurance company a letter that details what the policy limits for their liability coverage is and a statement that

103

you've settled your claim with that company for an amount that's equal to the limit of the policy as stated.

No-Fault Coverage will only pay for medical bills and lost income within the PIP benefits limits of your policy. In some states, after you file under the No-Fault insurance claim - referred to in the insurance policy as Personal Injury Protection (PIP) - you may also be entitled to file a liability claim against the person at fault. Such a liability claim will permit you to file against another driver in the accident to obtain compensation for medical and income losses over and above whatever the PIP benefit paid you as well as compensation for "pain and suffering." All of this to be executed exactly the same as a liability claim you would make in a state with a Fault Insurance system in effect.

## 5.  MEDICAL PAYMENTS COVERAGE

This optional coverage is purchased to pay your personal medical expenses plus those of your passengers, up to a certain amount, so stated on the policy. This coverage is often $1,000 to $5,000. It can sometimes be $50,000 or more. Medical payments will cover all medical bills up to the limits as stated in the policy, regardless of who's at fault.

## MED-PAY USUALLY COVERS:

1.  The medical expenses you or others may incur, up to the limits stated in the policy, for any person injured "in, around, above and below" your car.

2.  The medical expenses of any relative in your household who doesn't own a car, if they are injured either while riding in other motor vehicles, or struck by another car.

3.  Anyone driving your motor vehicle with your permission.

4.  The cost of an ambulance ride from the accident scene. There's also provisions for the funeral of the insured person who is involved in a fatal car accident. (Medical Payments Coverage is usually not required or necessary in No-Fault states, as detailed in CHAPTER 11).

## MEDICAL PAYMENTS PROVISIONS DO NOT COVER THE FOLLOWING SITUATIONS WHEN, AND IF, THEY NORMALLY OCCUR:

1. On a motorcycle, or any other two-wheeled vehicle, unless that vehicle is specifically listed in your policy.

2. While anyone was a passenger in a car owned by you or a relative, if that motor vehicle wasn't listed in your policy.

3. In a vehicle, other than a regular passenger car, if used for business.

4. During the course of your employment, if your injuries are also covered by worker's compensation laws.

5. You were driving another person's car, unless you've already claimed and collected the maximum of that car owner's Medical Payments Coverage. (In other words, if the Med-Pay Coverage isn't high enough on the person's motor vehicle you were operating you may proceed to collect from your own motor vehicle's Medical Payments Coverage, even though you were driving another car).

It's important that you're made aware of the fact that under Medical Payments Coverage, your insurance company often has the right to recover the amount of the medical payments made to you, if you also collected damages from a third source. For example, the liability insurance coverage from the company of the driver who hit you. If that's the case, when you receive a settlement from another source, you'll have to repay, out of that settlement, whatever dollar amounts you were paid under your own Medical Payments Coverage.

## READ, VERY CAREFULLY, ALL OTHER INSURANCE HEALTH POLICIES OR PLANS THAT MAY BE AVAILABLE TO YOU

It's possible to be reimbursed for your medical bills, yet avoid repayment, by implementing your non-automobile health insurance, or some other health plan that's available to you, instead of the Med-Pay coverage of your automobile insurance policy. Read, *very carefully*, your personal health policy/plan, or whatever other type of medical coverage you have. Your employer can provide you with a copy of the policy if you don't already have one.

If you have medical coverage you may decide to use it rather than the Medical Payments provision of your automobile insurance policy, because after reading the fine print you discover it's financially advantageous for you to do so. Does this mean there's a potential that you won't be required to pay the money back? That depends on the wording of the health policy/plan that's available to you.

105

# 6. ARBITRATION

*— this meaning is like mediation. Arbitration decision is final*

If you have a motor vehicle accident injury claim against your own insurance company, and all efforts have failed, your policy may allow you to take the matter to arbitration.

Arbitration is a procedure used to resolve disputes that has the informality of a Small Claims Court, but not its dollar ceiling, because the financial restrictions are determined by the limits stated in your insurance policy. Either you or your insurance company can initiate arbitration if it seems settlement negotiations have ground to a halt.

Both sides of the dispute explain their positions to a neutral individual, identified as the arbitrator. The insurance company must pay any amount the Arbitrator determines as fair compensation, within the limits of the policy. Their decision is almost always final and you must accept it.

## 6.1. Types Of Claims

Only certain types of motor vehicle accident claims filed under your own insurance policy must go to arbitration rather than to court:

1.     Most Uninsured Motorist Claims

2.     Most Underinsured Motorist Claims

3.     Some claims under Personal Injury Protection (PIP) policies in states with No-Fault insurance laws

To determine whether your claim must go to arbitration rather than court, examine your policy to see if there is an arbitration clause, how it works and how to proceed.

## 6.2. Issues To Be Resolved

It's true that fault is an issue that can be resolved in arbitration. However, since the main thrust of this book has nothing to do with fault, but everything to do with the evaluation of your "pain and suffering," the reader's interest and concern regarding arbitration is how much compensation is fair and reasonable for the injuries suffered and the income lost. The Arbitrator can award a dollar amount up to the limits of coverage as stated in your policy.

## 6.3. Procedure And Process

Who conducts the arbitration and where it takes place depends on the terms of your policy and on the arbitration laws in the state in which you live. Many arbitration clauses and state laws refer the matter to the American Arbitration Association, which has regional offices in many major cities and can arrange for an arbitration almost anywhere. Other laws refer people to a state or county arbitration board, or to an arbitration system administered by the state or county bar association.

Getting the arbitration process going requires a few simple steps, very much like the Small Claims Court procedure discussed in CHAPTER 10.

You can start arbitration proceedings by filing a written arbitration demand. This letter does not need to be in any particular form. Send it Certified Mail, Return Receipt Requested, to the adjuster you've been dealing with. Send a copy of that letter, Certified Mail, Return Receipt Requested, to the person in charge of the arbitration unit that will be handling your case. The letter should be set up something like this:

Date

Your full name
Street address
City/Town
State & Zip
Your telephone number
Fax number (if you have one)

Name of adjuster
Name of insurance company
Street address
City/Town
State & Zip

Re:    Claim number
       Date of loss
       (You should state) DEMAND FOR ARBITRATION

Dear:

This letter is my demand for arbitration of the above claim under the (Uninsured Coverage/Underinsured Coverage/Personal Injury Protection Coverage) of my (identify the name the insurance company) auto vehicle policy.

107

Spell out the relevant information as it applies to your claim as follows.

1.　　The policy number and coverage limits

2.　　The date and location of the accident

3.　　A brief description of the accident and an explanation of why there's no question that the other person was at fault

4.　　A summary description of your injuries, treatment and all possible or potential residual problems

5.　　The amount of income you lost

6.　　The property damage you sustained

7.　　The total amount you seek in compensation

[To determine what this figure should be, concentrate on the **BASE** "Value" you've worked out and decided to aim for, then multiply that figure by a minimum of two. So, if you've decided to aim for The Premium Value of $9,587.00 (a figure which, in this particular example, **BASE** has provided you with) your demand should be ($9,587.00 X 2) or at the very least $19,174.00, plus, if applicable, your Property Damage, whatever that was].

Having arrived at that figure the last line in your letter should be: "Compensation demand: Based on the above information, a fair and reasonable amount of compensation in the sum of . . . ." (Here you state the amount. In this example that figure would be $19,174.00 plus the amount of property damage).

## 6.4. Arbitration Fees

Arbitration fees are usually split evenly between the insurance company and the insured person. These fees normally cover the cost of arbitration, the hearing room and the paperwork involved. Any additional expenses you run up preparing for the arbitration must be paid by you.

Motor vehicle arbitration often takes several hours, but almost never more than half a day, and can cost several hundred dollars. Many arbitration associations require that the person who initiates arbitration must pay for half the administrative fees, up front. Be sure to check the fees procedure with the arbitration association you'll be dealing with before you start the process because the potential cost may be more than you're willing to spend.

## 6.5. The Hearing

Once the Arbitrator has been selected you'll be advised of the date, time and place of the arbitration hearing. At the hearing (much like what has already been explained and detailed in CHAPTER 10 regarding Small Claims Court Procedures) you'll have an opportunity to present all your documents to the Arbitrator and explain in your own words what happened in the accident, what your injuries are and how they have negatively affected your life. A representative of the insurance company, either an adjuster or a company lawyer, will present the company's side of the story. Your success in arbitration depends as much on how you prepare for it as on how you actually perform at the hearing.

## 6.6. Preparing The Documents

You do this the same way as was explained in CHAPTER 10 regarding Small Claims Court. Some Arbitrators want to have copies of all your documents before the arbitration. Others prefer to wait until the arbitration hearing begins. Check with the Arbitrator's office well before the date of your hearing to find out how that particular Arbitrator wants to proceed.

## 6.7. Preparing Your Statement

Once you're at the hearing you'll be able to speak to the Arbitrator informally, explaining your claim in plain language. Be sure to be emphatic about the pain, suffering and discomfort you had to deal with, the length of time it took you to fully recover and how your injuries affected your daily life. All of these critical areas have been touched upon and discussed, often in great depth, within the confines of this book. Just as for your presentation in Small Claims Court, you should prepare by making a list of the most important points, including:

1.    A description of the accident and why the other party is at fault

2.    A description of your injuries as demonstrated in your medical records

3.    Your documented property damages

4.    Your medical treatment and the length of your recovery

5.    The cost of your medical treatment

6.    The income you lost

7.    The non-medical losses you suffered, including any social, family, educational or other matters affected

Finally, you should be prepared to present the total compensation figure you believe is fair and reasonable. This should be the same amount as stated in the last paragraph in the settlement letter you sent to the insurance company in your demand. Try to keep your presentation to 15 or 20 minutes.

You may also bring a witness. A friend, family member or co-worker, who can add something to what you have to say and who will speak on your behalf is a valuable witness. This may be particularly useful if the witness can specifically address the issues of how profoundly you suffered from your injuries, how that pain affected you, your work and your social life.

A witness on your behalf who cannot, or will not, come to the arbitration in person may write a statement describing what their testimony would have been if they had actually appeared. That statement should include:

1. Their name and address

2. A declaration at the beginning: "If I were present in person at the arbitration, I would testify as follows."

3. A brief description of the point or points the witness can make on your behalf

4. A closing statement: "I declare under penalty of perjury under the laws of the state of (name the state) that the foregoing is true and correct."

5. The date

6. The witness' signature. Have his or her signature notarized. (Being notarized is not absolutely necessary because most Arbitrators will accept the statement even if it is not. However, it looks professional and much more official if it is).

## 6.8. The Decision

Within 30 days after the hearing, you and the insurance company will receive a written copy of the Arbitrator's decision. Both you and the insurance company must accept the Arbitrator's decision. If the Arbitrator awards you a specific amount of money, you should expect a check from the insurance company within two weeks.

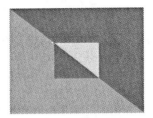

This now brings **AUTO ACCIDENT PERSONAL INJURY INSURANCE CLAIM** to a close.

I sincerely hope that The **BASE** Formula, together with the facts, data and insights, contained within this book, will prove to be of great profit to you.

*Dan Baldyga*

111

# Appendix A

### Initial Personal Checklist Regarding Your

Auto Accident Personal
Injury Insurance Claim

**Appendix A**

© 2002 Daniel G. Baldyga

[The reader will find a much more in-depth checklist contained in APPENDIX D as it specifically relates to CHAPTER THREE - GATHERING ACCIDENT FACTS].

The checklist below is simply a reminder, regarding information one should gather *immediately* after impact:

1.  Note the date, time and location of the accident.

2.  What was your destination? For what purpose?

3.  List the names, address and phone numbers of those who were in your vehicle at impact.

4.  Jot down the names, address and phone numbers of the driver(s) of all other vehicle(s) involved in the accident, as well as the same information about their passengers.

5.  What were the weather conditions?

6.  What were the traffic conditions?

7.  Were there any traffic control signals?

8.  What were the lighting conditions in the area where impact took place?

9.  Is it a residential, industrial or business district? City, urban or suburban?

10. Were there skid marks?

11. Try to obtain the names, addresses and telephone numbers of any uninvolved individuals who may have witnessed the accident.

## IF YOU'RE A PASSENGER:

a. Who was the driver at the wheel of each vehicle involved in the accident?

b. What is your relationship to the driver of the car you were in?

c. What was your sitting arrangement and position?

d. What was the nature of your trip? For what purpose was it being made? At whose invitation and for whose benefit?

e. Who invited you for the ride?

f. Had you ever rode with this driver before?

g. Did any of the other passenger(s) in the motor vehicle you were riding in voice any complaints or concerns regarding your drivers operating style during the course of the ride?

h. What was your previous knowledge of the driving ability or record of the person driving? Do you feel the driver operated his or her motor vehicle carefully or properly on this particular trip?

i. Had the driver, or anybody else in the motor vehicle, been drinking or taking drugs?

# Appendix B

Statues of Limitation

Auto Accident Personal
Injury Insurance Claim

**Appendix B**

© 2002 Daniel G. Baldyga

**Yearly Time-Limits for Starting of Action**

Listed below are the deadlines for negligence cases. The numbers refer to the years you have to file a lawsuit from the date of the accident. This table provides the general rule for filing most auto related, personal injury suits. The reader is cautioned and reminded that laws change. To be absolutely sure of your deadline you should double-check this information *in that state where the accident took place.*

|     | STATE                | PERSONAL INJURY | PROPERTY DAMAGE |
| --- | -------------------- | --------------- | --------------- |
| 1.  | Alabama              | 1               | 1               |
| 2.  | Alaska               | 2               | 6               |
| 3.  | Arizona              | 2               | 2               |
| 4.  | Arkansas             | 3               | 3               |
| 5.  | California           | 1               | 3               |
| 6.  | Colorado             | 6               | 6               |
| 7.  | Connecticut          | 2               | 2               |
| 8.  | Delaware             | 2               | 2               |
| 9.  | District of Columbia | 3               | 3               |
| 10. | Florida              | 4               | 3               |
| 11. | Georgia              | 2               | 4               |
| 12. | Hawaii               | 2               | 2               |
| 13. | Idaho                | 2               | 3               |
| 14. | Illinois             | 2               | 5               |
| 15. | Indiana              | 2               | 2               |

|  | STATE | PERSONAL | PROPERTY |
|---|---|---|---|
| 16. | Iowa | 2 | 5 |
| 17. | Kansas | 2 | 2 |
| 18. | Kentucky | 1 | 5 |
| 19. | Louisiana | 1 | 1 |
| 20. | Maine | 6 | 6 |
| 21. | Maryland | 3 | 3 |
| 22. | Massachusetts | 3 | 3 |
| 23. | Michigan | 3 | 3 |
| 24. | Minnesota | 6 | 6 |
| 25. | Mississippi | 6 | 6 |
| 26. | Missouri | 5 | 5 |
| 27. | Montana | 3 | 2 |
| 28. | Nebraska | 4 | 4 |
| 29. | Nevada | 2 | 3 |
| 30. | New Hampshire | 6 | 6 |
| 31. | New Jersey | 2 | 6 |
| 32. | New Mexico | 3 | 4 |
| 33. | New York | 3 | 3 |
| 34. | North Carolina | 3 | 3 |
| 35. | North Dakota | 6 | 6 |
| 36. | Ohio | 2 | 2 |
| 37. | Oklahoma | 2 | 2 |
| 38. | Oregon | 3 | 6 |

| | STATE | PERSONAL INJURY | PROPERTY DAMAGE |
|---|---|---|---|
| 39. | Pennsylvania | 2 | 6 |
| 40. | Rhode Island | 3 | 4 |
| 41. | South Carolina | 6 | 6 |
| 42. | South Dakota | 3 | 6 |
| 43. | Tennessee | 1 | 3 |
| 44. | Texas | 2 | 2 |
| 45. | Utah | 4 | 3 |
| 46. | Vermont | 3 | 3 |
| 47. | Virginia | 2 | 5 |
| 48. | Washington | 3 | 3 |
| 49. | West Virginia | 2 | 2 |
| 50. | Wisconsin | 3 | 6 |
| 51. | Wyoming | 4 | 4 |

As noted at several places in this book, this data was compiled in 1998 and 1999. Laws, rules and regulations change. To be absolutely sure that the above information is still accurate and up-to-date, you **must** double-check. The author and publisher acknowledge that the information is not necessarily current and that such information does change from time to time. As such, neither the author nor the publisher will accept any responsibility for the reader's reliance upon information contained in this book especially as regards such items as statues of limitations. The reader is urged to double check to ensure that he or she has the most current information.

# Appendix C
## Locating A Missing Witness

Auto Accident Personal
Injury Insurance Claim

**Appendix C**
© 2002 Daniel G. Baldyga

A witness can make or break a case. If you have a name, and you're trying to find that witness, but it seems that the individual has moved, or is no longer at the address you have, don't give up. Review the following . You may be able to find your witness:

1.  Send a Registered Letter, "Return Receipt Requested."

2.  Go through the telephone directories.

3.  Go through the city directories.

4.  Interview the janitor or landlord at the last known address for leads :

    a.  Names and addresses of relatives or friends.

    b.  Names of companies, agencies or bill collectors who may be looking for him. If you do turn one up, call and ask where he's now living.

    c.  Names of any fraternal, veterans or other organizations the witness may have belonged to. If you find he was a member of a union then call that particular union's local office and ask where he is now.

    d.  Interview the postman on that route. Check to see if he can provide you with some information, either a return mail address he may have noticed or perhaps he knows the witness's new address.

5.  Research the neighborhood or buildings for possible leads from friends, relatives or acquaintances. It's usually essential that such an investigation be repeated several times because you'll never find everyone home the first time the canvass is made, and there's always a possibility someone you saw previously has since seen or heard from the missing witness.

6.  Check the local churches and church organizations.

7.  Check local doctors and dentists who may have treated the witness.

8.  Visit the office personnel at the local parochial or public schools. The witnesses' children may have been transferred to another school and they'll surely have the new address information in their records.

9. Find out, through the neighbors, the name of a moving firm whose vehicles may have been observed moving the witness.

10. If you discover a former employer that's usually a home run. However, if they don't have a forwarding address, then ask about:

    a. Union affiliations.

    b. Names of references on employment records.

    c. Type of employment the witness will usually attempt to find.

    d. Talk to and ask for information from fellow workmen.

11. Automobile or motor vehicle bureaus may have some information concerning his address if an automobile has been registered in the witness' name, or if a driver or chauffeur's license was ever issued to him.

12. Local election records.

13. Utility and telephone companies.

14. Credit accounts at department stores.

15. Welfare agencies.

16. Military service or Veterans Administration records.

17. Is there a policeman on that beat? Question him, using all of the above suggested leads.

18. Tax records.

19. Check with golf, tennis or other athletic clubs that the witness may have belonged to, including leads through any hobbies the witness may have had.

20. Talk to the owner and employees at the nearest barber shop or beauty salon and/or package store.

21. One of the best places to obtain information about a missing witness is at the local pubs. People spend many hours sipping and chatting. Check with the owner, the bartenders and the regular customers.

# Appendix D
## After Impact Checklist

Auto Accident Personal
Injury Insurance Claim

**Appendix D**
© 2002 Daniel G. Baldyga

1.  Draw as complete a diagram of the scene of the accident as possible, including, as best you can determine, the position of all vehicles before, during and after impact. Include the measurement of street, traffic lanes, distance from the curb or shoulder, skid marks, distance from lights and intersections, positions of all skid marks or debris on the road or shoulders, etc.

2.  Snap photographs of impact area as detailed in CHAPTER 3.

3.  Record the weather conditions at the time of the accident:

    a.  Was there snow, rain, hail, fog, mist, sleet, wind?

    b.  Was the windshield wiper working?

    c.  Was the sun in the other operator's face?

4.  Jot down a complete description of road conditions:

    a.  Dry, wet, slippery, icy, etc.

    b.  Smooth, rough, bumpy, ruts, etc.

5.  Descriptions of streets, roads and/or highways:

    a.  Describe marks, gouges, or debris on the street, road or shoulders.

    b.  BE SURE TO SNAP PHOTOGRAPHS OF SKID MARKS AND/OR IMPACT GOUGES ON ROAD SURFACE!

    c.  Describe the area : City, urban, suburban, business, factory.

    d.  Was the road crowned or flat?

    e.  Was the road straight or curved?

    f.  Was the road paved with macadam, asphalt, concrete, cobblestone, brick, gravel or dirt?

g.      Was the road level or inclined?

h.      Measure the width of the roads or streets and the number of lanes. Where they marked? Describe markings.

i.      Did the street contain rail or trolley tracks?

j.      Measure the width, depth and general nature of any ditches.

k.      Also measure the width, construction and type of shoulders.

l.      Describe and photograph the location as to general visibility, and list obstructions (parked vehicles, buildings, trees shrubbery).

6.    Traffic controls:

a.      Was a police officer directing traffic?

b.      Were there any traffic lights or signals at the location of the scene? Were they in operation? Give exact location.

c.      Describe any stop signs or other warning signs and jot down their exact location.

d.      Did the accident take place in a hospital or school zone and were signs posted?

e.      Was the road posted with relation to speed?

7.    Description of skid marks:

a.      Exact location.

b.      Measurements.

c.      Direction.

d.      Review CHAPTER 3 regarding photographs/skid marks

8.  Description of any debris at the scene.

a.      Glass, oil stains, parts of the automobile(s).

b.      Exact location.

9. Complete description of the lighting situation:

   a. Daylight, dusk, cloudy, night, moonlight? Include the position of the sun to indicate in which direction it was shining.

   b. Headlights: Bright, medium, dim, parking. Fog lights?

   c. Were approaching headlights blinding? Was traffic heavy?

   d. Road or street lights? Give exact power and distances as nearly as possible.

   e. Were flares needed? Where they available? Where were they placed? Were they set up properly?

10. Condition of car that struck you:

    a. Age and general care given it.

    b. Take photographs of all vehicles, as detailed in CHAPTER 3.

    c. Check out and gather information on any specific items that may not have been functioning correctly and may have contributed to the accident such as brakes, headlights, directional signals, tires, tail lights, horn, steering, etc. Were chains or snow tires used or necessary? If so what condition where they in?

    Note: If you have reason to believe that one of the above mentioned items may have been the cause of the accident, either directly or indirectly, find out when that motor vehicle was last checked, where and by whom? This information can often be found by opening the vehicle's door and locating the sticker placed there by the garage that last worked on it.

11. Determine whether there was any state inspection of the other vehicle. If so, when and where? (Simply read the State Inspection Sticker usually placed on the motor vehicle's windshield). You may find that the vehicle was operating without having complied with local inspection regulations or that the car has been rejected, for any number of reasons, and that the defect for which it was rejected has not yet been repaired. If so you'll have enhanced your position because this may constitute some evidence of negligence, provided that such a violation contributed to the accident.

12. Document a complete description of the area, including the location of all

buildings that might house possible witnesses.

13.    Be sure to obtain the names, addresses and phone numbers, both business and home, of any and all independent witnesses who were not involved in the accident.

14.    Jot down the details of what happened to your body at impact plus every physical sensation you felt. Describe as clearly as possible where, how and to what degree the pain was that you experienced.

15.    Describe any medical treatment you have initially received on an emergency, or other basis, following the accident. Try to obtain the names, addresses, job titles and phone numbers of those who attended you.

16.    If you were transported from the scene of the accident by ambulance try to find and interview the attendants and drivers. If possible take their statements. Describe in detail, in their written statements, the location of the accident-related vehicles, whatever skid marks they may have observed and also any admissions of fault made by the driver and/or the passenger(s) in the motor vehicle that smashed into you.

17.    If vehicles were removed by a wrecker or towing company, see if you can find and interview the wrecker's driver and take his statement. Try to capture his observations regarding after-accident details. For example, skid, drag and/or gouge marks, location of debris, condition of the other vehicle's brake lights, horns, or tires, and the extent of damage to the vehicles. Ask him about statements or admissions by the drivers, or any others, who may have been involved in the accident, etc.

18.    Jot down the negligent party's comportment, actions, reactions and inactions, plus any statements he may have made, and to whom.

19.    Obtain the file number designated by the police for the accident .

## A SPECIAL NOTE

You may wonder, "If I'm not liable for this accident and I know I'm going to be paid anyway, why in the world should I put myself through all this extra work, chasing down this information"?    The answer to that is "cash."  When you're not responsible for the accident you were in, it does take a great deal of effort to gather up this additional data - especially when you know you're going to be reimbursed for your loss. *However*, when it comes to the results you're going to obtain from **The BASE Formula**, it's crucial that you accumulate as many facts as possible. If you do, it will almost always justify moving your settlement figure *upwards* and aiming for a higher "Value." For example, let's assume that **The BASE Formula** provided you with the following four "Values":

122

| | |
|---|---|
| A PREMIUM Value of | $15,504.00 |
| A MEAN Value of | $12,920.00 |
| A CORE Value of | $11,628.00 |
| A LOW Value of | $ 7,752.00 |

After reviewing these four "Values" you're confident that under normal circumstances, on a loss with your particular damages, The MEAN Value of $12,920.00 rests comfortably within the area of what your claim is routinely worth.

But, you have photographs of the vehicle that hit you. They clearly indicate it's a rusty pile of junk with previously smashed, yet unrepaired damage, driven on tires so bald the thread is almost invisible. Plus, you have proof positive that when the accident occurred the weather was so bad that the person who struck you was clearly driving much too fast for existing conditions.

You have a copy of the police report which indicates 127 feet of skid marks the bucket-of-bolts left behind it prior to impact. In addition to all that, you've secured a statement from an independent witness who observes, "That guy was going like a bat out of hell! Later on I saw him stumbling around the accident scene. He looked to me like he'd been boozing it up."

After you've presented all of the above to the adjuster he'll return to his office where he'll review the various information you've provided him with. Then he'll sit down with his supervisor, hand him what you've accumulated and exclaim, "What this claimant has put together makes our insured look *pretty bad.*"

His supervisor responds, "Man, if a judge or jury ever got their hands on these photographs and documents we could get *killed!* I mean, *buried alive!*" At that point the "Value" of your claim has suddenly escalated. In the circumstances as detailed above, it moved from The MEAN Value of $12,920.00 *up* to The PREMIUM Value of $15,504.00. Maybe ten, fifteen or even twenty percent more! You'll find out when you begin to negotiate. And that's the reason you should consider doing all this extra work.

By demonstrating to the adjuster that you've gathered such potent information you're in a much better position to move from one "Value" *up* to another than if you hadn't gone through the effort of collecting such devastating facts. This is especially true if the information is damaging to his insured and would look deplorable should the case ever end up in a court of law.

# Appendix E

Sample Lost Wage & Earning Verification Document

Auto Accident Personal Injury Insurance Claim

**Appendix E**

© 2002 Daniel G. Baldyga

To prove your lost work and earnings, either full or part time, you must obtain a Lost Wage and Earning Verification letter. It should be signed by the proper individual within the corporation, company or organization you're employed by, on their official letterhead, which covers the following:

1. Your full name, address and Social Security number.

2. Full name and address of your employer.

3. Date you were first employed.

4. Your present title, or job description.

5. Whether you were paid or not, list the dates you were unable to work:

   From: _____       To: _____

6. Average weekly wage/salary:  $ _____

7. If you believe it has a bearing on your claim, ask your employer to verify in writing that during the period you were unable to work you were deprived of:

   a. Commissions lost - Amount: $ _____

   b. Overtime lost - Amount: $ _____

   c. Tips and gratuities lost - Amount: $ _____

   d. Bonus lost - Amount: $ _____

8.  Ask your employer to include in this Lost Wage And Earning Document a detailed statement regarding your regular duties.

9.  If applicable you should have your employer state in writing:

    a.  How much vacation time you lost.

    b.  How much sick leave you lost.

    c.  Was there a loss of future earning capacity? Explain.

    d.  State in detail if you were absent from any important business or sales meetings.

10. Ask your employer to be sure, at the end of the Lost Wage And Earnings document, that it's clearly stated:

    a.  Who signed it.

    b.  Their title.

    c.  The date it was signed.

Once the above has been accomplished you should document all personal out-of-pocket expenses for:

1.  Child care.

2.  Household help.

3.  Travel to and from medical care.

Also, if applicable, state details regarding:

1.  Any missed appointments with clients and/or potential customers? If so, list and explain.

2.  Document any interviews and/or opportunities you lost that may have led to a better job.

| Appendix F | Auto Accident Personal Injury Insurance Claim |
|---|---|
| **Appendix F** Self Employment Affidavit | **Appendix F** © 2002 Daniel G. Baldyga |

If you're self-employed this is a suggested sample of an affidavit you should create, execute and have notarized.

## AFFIDAVIT OF SELF-EMPLOYMENT

STATE OF: _____

COUNTY OF: _____

I, Mr/Mrs/Ms _____being first duly sworn, depose and state as follows under oath:

1. That I reside at: _____

2. That on:_____I was involved in an accident which occurred at the

   following location: _____

3. That as a result of said accident, I was unable to work.

   From:_____To: _____

4. That at the time of the accident, I was self-employed as: _____ under the business name of:

   _____ Located at:

   _____

5. During that period of time my average earnings per week were: $_____

6. Because I was unable to work, I lost income for the said period of disability in the amount of: $_____

   Date: _____, 20 ____      Signature:

   _____

Subscribed and sworn before me this _____ day of _____,

20_____


_____

Notary Public



In addition to the notarized affidavit above, and if applicable, the following should be considered:

1.  Be ready to supply a detailed report which will prove the cost to you for any and all additional help you needed to hire while you were undergoing medical treatment or recuperating.

2.  To help substantiate what is stated in the affidavit you should have available copies of your prior years Federal and State income tax returns.

3.  If your business lost money while you were laid up you should determine how much and be prepared to present documents to prove your loss.

4.  Providing copies of documents proving business meetings or appointments you had to cancel while you were recuperating which negatively impacted your present or future income.

127

# Appendix G
## Checklist of Personal Injury Damages

1.     PAST MEDICAL EXPENSES:

    a.     Names of Physicians & Surgeons:
        Charge/Cost $ _____

    b.     Names of Hospitals Involved:
        Charge/Cost $ _____

    c.     Diagnostic Tests. (X-Rays/CT Scan, etc.):
        Charge/Cost $ _____

    d.     Laboratory Services. Urinalysis, Blood Test, Serological Tests, EKG, EEG, Ultrasound, etc.):
        Charge/Cost $ _____

    e.     Ambulance Services:
        Charge/Cost $ _____

    f.     Emergency Room Care:
        Charge/Cost $ _____

    g.     Over-The-Counter Medications:
        Charge/Cost $ _____

    h.     Prescription Medications:
        Charge/Cost $ _____

    i.     Dentists:
        Charge/Cost $ _____

    j.     Chiropractors:
        Charge/Cost $ _____

    k.     Medical Consultants:
        Charge/Cost $ _____

    l.     Other Past Medical Expenses:
        Charge/Cost $ _____

2. POST-INJURY REHABILITATIVE CARE:

    a.    Physical Therapy:
            Charge/Cost $ _____

    b.    Prosthetic Devises & Related Equipment. (Cane, Crutch/Neck Brace/Ace Bandage, etc.):
            Charge/Cost $ _____

3. EXPENSES RELATED TO MEDICAL CARE:

    a.    Private Nursing Care:
            Charge/Cost $ _____

    b.    Travel Expenses:
            Charge/Cost $ _____

    c.    Lodging Expenses:
            Charge/Cost $ _____

    d.    Telephone Expenses:
            Charge/Cost $ _____

    e.    Baby Sitting Expenses:
            Charge/Cost $ _____

    f.    Rental Equipment:
            Charge/Cost $ _____

    g.    Specially Equipped Vehicles:
            Charge/Cost $ _____

4. EXPLAIN AND PROVE POTENTIAL FUTURE MEDICAL EXPENSES:

    a.    Physical Therapy and/or Rehabilitative Expenses.

    b.    Physician, Chiropractor, and Related Medical Expenses.

    c.    Hospitalization. (For what services and the expected duration).

129

                d.      Diagnostic Tests.


        5.      DOCUMENT:

                a.      Contention of a Permanent Disability.

                b.      Contention of a period of Temporary Disability. (Length of time).

                c.      That period of time you endured TOTAL DISABILITY because of the accident.

                d.      That period of time you endured PARTIAL DISABILITY because of the accident.

                e.      Visible Scarring.

                f.      Physical Deformities.


## DESCRIBE IN WRITING THE  PHYSICAL "PAIN AND SUFFERING" YOU ARE EXPERIENCING

If at all possible, keep a diary to refer to at a later date. Or have someone else keep the diary for you, if you are unable to. Express the pain you feel, where it's coming from and how long it lasts. This may become very important should you find yourself on a witness stand, four or five years down the road. Having your diary to refer to will be very helpful.

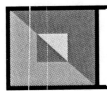
\* Data Compiled 1999 so you must double check these figures

| State | Amount | State | Amount |
|---|---|---|---|
| Alabama | $3,000.00 | Missouri | $3,500.00 |
| Alaska | $7,500.00 | Montana | $3,000.00 |
| Arizona | $2,500.00 | Nebraska | $2,100.00 |
| Arkansas | $5,000.00 | Nevada | $3,500.00 |
| California | $5,000.00 | New Hampshire | $5,000.00 |
| Colorado | $5,000.00 | New Jersey | $2,000.00 |
| Connecticut | $2,500.00 | New Mexico | $5.000.00 |
| Delaware | $15,000.00 | New York | $3,000.00 |
| D.C. | $5,000.00 | North Carolina | $3,000.00 |
| Florida | $5,000.00 | North Dakota | $5,000.00 |
| Georgia | $5,000.00 | Ohio | $3,000.00 |
| Hawaii | $3,500.00 | Oklahoma | $4,500.00 |
| Idaho | $3,000.00 | Oregon | $3,500.00 |
| Illinois | $5,000.00 | Pennsylvania | $8,000.00 |
| (Cook County) | $2,500.00 | (Philadelphia) | $6.500.00 |
| Indiana | $3,000.00 | Rhode Island | $1,500.00 |
| (Marion & Lake County) $6,000.00 | | South Carolina | $5,000.00 |
| Iowa | $4,000.00 | South Dakota | $4,000.00 |
| Kansas | $1,800.00 | Tennessee (*) | $15,000.00 |
| Kentucky | $1,500.00 | Texas | $5,000.00 |
| Louisiana | $3,000.00 | Utah | $5,000.00 |
| Maine | $4,500.00 | Vermont | $3,500.00 |
| Maryland | $2,500.00 | Virginia | $15,000.00 |
| Massachusetts | $2,000.00 | Washington | $2,500.00 |
| Michigan | $3,000.00 | West Virginia | $5,000.00 |
| Minnesota | $7,500.00 | Wisconsin | $5,000.00 |
| Mississippi | $2,500.00 | Wyoming | $3,000.00 |

(*) $25,000 in counties with populations greater than 700,000

**As noted this data was compiled in 1999. Laws, rules and regulations change. To be sure of current small claims dollar limits you must double-check to confirm the legal limits.**

131

# INDEX

# About The Author

Auto Accident Personal
Injury Insurance Claim

Daniel G. Baldyga
© 2002

## Daniel G. Baldyga

Dan Baldyga has a lifetime of experience in the field of motor vehicle accidents, personal injury and compensation. He worked his way through college employed by a detective agency, where his assignments included insurance fraud, missing persons, financial and background investigations and undercover operations. He specialized in representing major New England insurance companies, for whom he collected evidence in the inquiry of automobile accidents.

Upon graduation, Baldyga joined the United States Navy and was assigned to the Special Unit in Criminal Investigations, where his primary duty was to travel throughout the Midwest, determining negligence and bringing to a conclusion those accident cases involving government motor vehicles.

After serving in the Navy, he entered the world of insurance claims, where he worked as an adjuster, was promoted to supervisor, and then to claims manager. He spent the last five years of his career assisting company attorneys at court trials.

In 1968, Baldyga wrote the ground-breaking *How To Settle Your Own Insurance Claim,* published by Macmillan. This revolutionary concept to assist laymen with their insurance claims created a heated debate within both the insurance and legal industries -- because it revealed, for the first time, the secrets surrounding the settlement of motor vehicle accident claims. This had never been done before!

135

© 1999-2003 Daniel G. Baldyga

Baldyga appeared on over 100 regional and national television and radio talk shows throughout the United States. His innovative book sold 57,000 copies. His publications also include the (1983) novel, *A Sailor Remembers,* and his second "how-to" insurance claim guide *Secrets Never Told,* released in 1998. He is a featured columnist and his insurance claim articles appear in various publications reaching millions of readers each year.

Upon his retirement, Baldyga decided that it was time to publish the *definitive* self-help guide concerning motor vehicle accident personal injury claims. After examining mountains of statistics and confidential reports he has created the **Baldyga Auto Accident Settlement Evaluation (BASE) Formula**. Experts have called this personal injury evaluation method "amazing" and "revolutionary." **The BASE Formula** is ingenious yet matter-of-fact, simple, yet accurate, and it eliminates the mystery of how to place a monetary value on "pain and suffering."

In his new book, ***Auto Accident Personal Injury Insurance Claim***, Baldyga has once again broken new ground in the normally dormant, unchanging landscape of motor vehicle accident insurance claims – and helped tip the balance from the insurance companies to the consumer.